100 THINGS TO DO IN KNOXVILLE BEFORE YOU DIE

Putting the TRAVEL in NTTW! ~Kristen

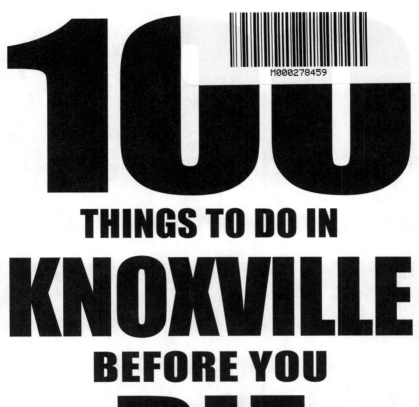

Sunsphere in World's Fair Park. Courtesy of Visit Knoxville

100
THINGS TO DO IN
KNOXVILLE
BEFORE YOU
DIE

KRISTEN COMBS

REEDY PRESS

Reedy Press
PO Box 5131
St. Louis, MO 63139, USA
www.reedypress.com

Library of Congress Control Number: 2022949241

ISBN: 9781681064239

Design by Jill Halpin

All photos are by the author unless otherwise noted.
Cover image courtesy of Steven Bearden.

Printed in the United States of America
23 24 25 26 27   5 4 3 2 1

DEDICATION

To Jeff and Lily, who put up with my shenanigans.

WELCOME
All Sizes
ALL COLORS
ALL AGES
ALL SEXES
ALL CULTURES
ALL All types
RELIGIONS
All Beliefs · All People
SAFE HERE AT
Yassin's FALAFEL HOUSE

Yassin's Falafel House

CONTENTS

Preface .... **xiii**

Acknowledgments .... **xv**

Food and Drink

1. Find Your Favorite BBQ **2**

2. Track Down a Food Truck **4**

3. Make a Choice at a Meat and Three **5**

4. Go from Farm to Table **6**

5. "Gas Up" at Petro's Chili & Chips **7**

6. Travel the Globe with International Cuisine **8**

7. Have a Nice Day at the Nicest Place in America **10**

8. Traverse the Ale Trail **12**

9. Catch a Skyline Sunset from a Rooftop Bar **14**

10. Make a Toast to the Tennessee Whiskey Trail **16**

11. Scream for Ice Cream at the Phoenix Pharmacy and Cruze Farm **17**

12. Fill Your Tote Bag at the Market Square Farmers Market **18**

13. Eat Your Way through Knoxville on a Food Tour **19**

14. Sip in a Swing at K Brew **20**

15. Dust Off Your Spurs at Lonesome Dove **22**

16. Lay Down the Law at Saloon 16 .... **23**

17. Lift Your Pinky at THE TENNESSEAN **24**

18. Consume Cocktails in Concealment **25**

19. Go Forth, Go North in North Knoxville **26**

20. Surf the South Coast in South Knoxville **28**

21. Watch the Process at Pretentious Craft Co. **30**

22. Taste Tennessee at Tsali Notch Winery **31**

Music and Entertainment

23. Give Regards to Broadway at the Tennessee Theatre **34**

24. Shine Bright at the Bijou Theatre **35**

25. Get Down at the Clarence Brown Theatre **36**

26. Break a Leg at the Knoxville Children's Theatre **37**

27. Dance a Jig at Boyd's Jig and Reel **38**

28. Hoot 'n' Holler at the WDVX Blue Plate Special **39**

29. See a Show at the Theatre Knoxville Downtown **40**

30. Unite in Storytelling at the River & Rail Theatre **41**

31. Rock Out at the School of Music **42**

32. Fiddle Around on the Cradle of Country Music Tour **43**

33. Tune into the Knoxville Symphony Orchestra **44**

34. Unpack Your Bags at the Carpetbag Theatre **45**

35. C'mon Get Happy in Central/Happy Holler **46**

36. Listen Up at Big Ears **47**

37. Open Up to the Opera at the Rossini Festival **48**

38. Be Merry and Go Round at the Tennessee Valley Fair **49**

Sports and Recreation

39. Sing "Rocky Top" at a UT Football Game **52**

40. Head into the Urban Wilderness **53**

41. Be One with Nature at Ijams Nature Center **54**

42. Go Your Own Way on a Greenway **55**

43. Shout "Let's Go, Ice Bears!" at a Knoxville Ice Bears Hockey Game... **56**

44. Shoot Hoops at the Women's Basketball Hall of Fame **57**

45. Tell a Secret at the Knoxville Botanical Garden **58**

46. Pack a Picnic at UT Gardens **60**

47. Paddle the Tennessee River **62**

48. Cruise the Tennessee River **63**

49. Spare an Afternoon at Maple Hall **64**

50. Swing through the Trees at Navitat **65**

51. All You Have to Do Is Dream at Everly Brothers Park **66**

52. Choose an Event at Chilhowee Park **67**

53. Lace Up for a Walk at Lakeshore Park **68**

54. Take a Hike at House Mountain **69**

55. Kick It at a One Knoxville Soccer Game **70**

56. Take Me Out to the Ball Game at the Tennessee Smokies 71

57. Be A-MAZE-D at Maple Lane Farms 72

58. Do It Your Way in the Great Smoky Mountains National Park 73

Culture and History

59. Hold Down the Fort at James White's Fort 76

60. Get Constitutional at Blount Mansion 77

61. Have a Bonny Good Time at Marble Springs 78

62. Look around the River Bend at Crescent Bend 79

63. Think Pink (or Blue) at Historic Ramsey House 80

64. Avoid a Scandal at Mabry-Hazen House and Bethel Cemetery 82

65. Follow Your (He)Art at Historic Westwood 83

66. Go Back in Time at the East Tennessee History Center 84

67. Go Back Further in Time at the McClung Museum 85

68. Preserve African American History at the Beck Cultural Exchange Center 86

69. Carve Out an Afternoon at Candoro Marble Building 87

70. Wig Out at the Sunsphere 88

71. Divide and Conquer on the Civil War Driving Tour 90

72. Get Your Steps In with Knoxville Walking Tours 91

73. Events below Earth at Cherokee Caverns 92

74. Open Your Eyes at the Knoxville Museum of Art 93

75. Hunt for Murals 94

76. Search for Sculptures, Statues, and Memorials **95**

77. Proceed to Read with Knoxville's Literary Connections **96**

78. Have a Wildly Fun Time at Zoo Knoxville **98**

79. Learn the Power of Play at Muse Knoxville... **99**

80. Ace the Test on the University of Tennessee Campus **100**

81. All Aboard! The Three Rivers Rambler **102**

82. Full Speed Ahead at the Farragut Museum..**103**

83. Twist and Turn on the French Broad Driving Tour..............................**104**

84. Bark and Howl at Mardi Growl...**105**

85. Celebrate Arts, Culture, and Natural Beauty with Dogwood Arts........**106**

86. Party around the Globe without Leaving Town **108**

87. Salute a Soldier at the Veterans Day Parade..**109**

88. Celebrate Christmas in the City **110**

89. Keep the Past Alive at the Museum of Appalachia..............................**111**

90. Day Trip to Historic Clinton **112**

91. Keep a Secret in the Secret City...**113**

Shopping and Fashion

92. Look Up on the Downtown Walking Tour **116**

93. Take Heart for Art on First Friday **118**

94. Make Haste to the Maker City **120**

95. Shop from Yesteryear at Mast General Store **121**

96. Get Groovy at Knoxville's Vintage Stores **122**

97. To Market, to Market in Market Square **124**

98. Go West, Young Man, to West Knoxville **125**

99. Shop 'Til You Drop in Bearden **126**

100. Sneak through Sutherland Avenue **128**

Activities by Season **131**

Suggested Itineraries **135**

Index **139**

PREFACE

Having spent the past several years of my career at Visit Knoxville, I am intensely focused on the visitor experience in this city. In writing this book, I know it's not just visitors who need help in planning their vacations, but natives and recent transplants are also always looking for things to do in the place they call home.

Knoxville is a slice of Americana; its history goes back to the Cherokee and Indigenous peoples prior to European settlement west of the Appalachians, spanning the contentious Civil War and rise to industry, resulting in a modern city full of surprises.

Visitors and locals alike ask me what there is to do here, and I flip the question back: Do you love the great outdoors? Want to try new things? Enjoy galleries and theater? It may sound cliché, but Knoxville has it all, and that's where this list of 100 things comes in.

My hope is you'll approach this guide with gusto and fall in love with Knoxville, a nature-loving-adventure-seeking-artsy kinda town!

Kristen Combs

Historic Westwood

ACKNOWLEDGMENTS

My sincerest thanks to my colleagues and friends at Visit Knoxville, especially to Kim Bumpas and Angie Wilson for their encouragement and unwavering support. My deepest appreciation goes to all the wonderful people in tourism and hospitality I've had the pleasure to work with over the years—I hope you'll read this and know who you are. Thank you for making Knoxville an incredible place to visit AND call home!

PostModern Spirits. Courtesy of Aaron Russel

FOOD AND DRINK

1

FIND
YOUR FAVORITE BBQ

Planted firmly in the South, Knoxville is expected to have decent barbecue—and we do! Sweet P's is one of the most well-known barbecue joints, featured from Travel Channel's *Man v. Food* to the Food Network and beyond. The downtown location was born from a love of classic American dive bars and a love for the 1982 World's Fair. I always split the sampler. At Archer's BBQ, expect to find a dry-rub style, as the owner and chef hails from Memphis. Archer's sides are equally good; I can't get enough of the loaded potato salad. Oakwood BBQ is a food truck with the best combo of meat and three. It's in their "Meaty Mac," and you're guaranteed to enjoy this marriage of brisket and gooey mac 'n' cheese. At Dead End, they claim you have arrived at the end of your search for great barbecue in East Tennessee. You can be the judge if your own journey stops here, but there's more barbecue to be had in this town.

Sweet P's BBQ
3029 Tazewell Pike, 865-437-3974
410 W Jackson Ave., 865-281-1738
sweetpbbq.com

Archers BBQ
5415 Kingston Pike, 865-394-9580
10225 Chapman Hwy., Seymour, 865-771-9389
1301 E Emory Rd., 865-687-2694
10205 Kingston Pike, 865-771-2601
5200 Rutledge Pike, 865-722-1989
archersbbq.com

Oakwood BBQ
facebook.com/oakwoodbbqknox

Dead End BBQ
3621 Sutherland Ave., 865-212-5655
deadendbbq.com

2

TRACK DOWN
A FOOD TRUCK

The problem of having a group agree on what to eat is solved with a food truck park, because everyone can get what they want. Knoxville has several scattered throughout town, so you're never far from a soon-to-be-satisfied stomach. Central Filling Station was the first food truck park to be established, close to the Happy Holler neighborhood. Depending on the day and time, expect up to four trucks in what was once an old gas station on Central Avenue. Plan around trivia night or live music for an entertainment bonus. On the south side of the river, check out the aptly named SouthSide Garage. Similarly, this was once a mechanics garage on Sevier Avenue. Today, you'll often find a resident food truck and a rotating option, an inside bar serving craft beer and cocktails, and dining space indoors and out. No hibernating at the Cave, serving up food-truck options beside Hey Bear Cafe, the town's hottest spot for boba tea in West Knoxville.

Central Filling Station
900 N Central St.
knoxfoodpark.com

SouthSide Garage
1014 Sevier Ave., 865-951-2790
southsidegarageknox.com

The Cave at Hey Bear Cafe
9036 Middlebrook Pike, 865-985-0326
heybearcafe.com

3

MAKE A CHOICE
AT A MEAT AND THREE

The meat and three (also called a blue plate special) is a Southern specialty, and did you know its roots can be traced to the state of Tennessee? For those unfamiliar, these restaurants typically offer a rotating daily selection of choice of meat such as fried chicken, meat loaf, or country fried steak along with a few sides such as mashed potatoes, green beans, collard greens, and macaroni and cheese. Frequently associated with soul food, these dining establishments are easy to find throughout Knoxville. Most serve comforting flavors, but for those who can take some heat, give Jackie's version of Nashville hot chicken a try. Be warned, hot is hot!

Jackie's Dream
1008 E Woodland Ave., 865-219-5789
jackiesdreamknoxville.com

The Lunch House
3816 Holston Dr., 865-637-5188

Pete's Restaurant
540 Union Ave., 865-523-2860
petescoffeeshop.com

Round Up Restaurant and Ice Cream
3643 Sevierville Pike, 865-577-8981
round-up-restaurant-and-ice-cream.business.site

4

GO FROM
FARM TO TABLE

Many restaurants in Knoxville pride themselves on farm-fresh ingredients, taking care to share the specific farms and product partners on their menus and websites. Chef Joseph Lenn, Tennessee's first James Beard Award winner, operates J. C. Holdway, another standout that lists Cruze Farm, Marsh Hen Mill, Sunburst Trout Farms, and Vienna Coffee Company, among others. Chef Jeffrey DeAlejandro, owner of breakfast hot spot OliBea, features Tellico Plains Bakery, Circle V Farms, Zavels Family Farm, Abbey Field Farm, and more. Market Square icon Oliver Royale shines with Mossy Creek Farms, Mountain Meadows Fram, West Wind Farms, Lacewing Farms, Knox CityFarm, and Seven Springs Farm. From barn to bistro, dine at some of Knoxville's finest tables.

J. C. Holdway
501 Union Ave., 865-312-9050
jcholdway.com

OliBea
211 S Central St., 865-200-5450
olibeaoldcity.com

Oliver Royale
5 Market Sq., 865-622-6434
oliverroyale.com

5

"GAS UP"
AT PETRO'S CHILI & CHIPS

Nashville has hot chicken, Memphis battles Kansas City over the best barbecue, and Philly has the ubiquitous cheesesteak. But does Knoxville have a culinary icon? Even locals miss one right under their nose—the "Petro." What was first called a "Petroleum Belly" debuted at the 1982 World's Fair in Knoxville (more on that later). The theme of that exposition was Energy, and this unique grab-n-go dish was guaranteed to power-up! The Petro consisted of a bag of Fritos® topped with chili and layered with cheddar and jack cheese, diced tomatoes, green onions, and sour cream. You can try Petro's Chili & Chips downtown in Market Square or in select locations in Tennessee, Arkansas, and North Carolina. Be sure to enjoy yours with a Hint-of-Orange Iced Tea!

2 Market Sq., 865-444-3970
petros.com

TRAVEL THE GLOBE
WITH INTERNATIONAL CUISINE

We've covered the Southern staples—but there's more than biscuits and gravy! For some European flair, try crêpes at the French Market Crêperie or bouillabaisse at Northshore Brasserie. Visit Emilia in Market Square or Savelli's on Sutherland for Italian. Schulzes Schnitzel Kitchen pairs German pretzels with Hefeweizen, and the Jig and Reel's Scottish menu meets its match with fine scotch. Say "slainte" at the Irish pub Clancy's, and Kefi is the perfect homage to Greek cuisine. Vegans can compare falafel at KoPita and Yassin's Falafel House. Gosh Ethiopian Restaurant is another vegan-friendly spot. Asia is represented too, from Vietnam with Bida Saigon, Thailand with Surin of Thailand, Cambodia with the Landing House, Laos with Sticky Rice Cafe, Japan with Nama and Kaizen, and India with Tandur and Sitar. Move to Latin America for a taste of Brazil with Brazeiros. I could fill a book with Mexican restaurants, but I'll stick with my personal fave: Taqueria La Herradura. Salud!

The French Market Crêperie
412 Clinch Ave., 865-540-4372
thefrenchmarketknoxville.com

Northshore Brasserie
9430 S Northshore Dr., 865-539-5188
northshorebrasserie.com

Emilia
16 Market Sq., 865-313-2472
emiliaknox.com

Savelli's
3055 Sutherland Ave., 865-521-9085
savellisknoxville.com

Schulzes Schnitzel Kitchen
126 Bernard Ave., 865-415-3845
schulzesschnitzelkitchen.com

Boyd's Jig and Reel
101 S Central St., 865-247-7066
jigandreel.com

Clancy's
602 S Gay St., 865-219-1266
clancystavern.com

Kefi
120 E Jackson Ave., 865-544-8564
kefiknox.com

KoPita
507 S Gay St., 865-249-8823
kopitarestaurants.com

Yassin's Falafel House
706 Walnut St., 865-219-1462
yassinsfalafelhouse.com

Bida Saigon
8078 Kingston Pike, 865-694-5999
bidasaigoncafe.com

Surin of Thailand
6213 Kingston Pike, 865-330-0007
surinofthailand.com

The Landing House
1147 Sevier Ave., 865-249-7424
landinghouse-109226.square.site

Sticky Rice Cafe
120 Jack Dance St., 865-249-6273
stickyriceknox.com

Nama Sushi Bar
506 S Gay St., 865-633-8539
namasushibar.com

Kaizen
127 S Central St., 865-409-4444
knoxkaizen.com

Tandur
6502 Kingston Pike, 865-249-7254
tandur.com

Sitar
6004 Kingston Pike, 865-588-1828
sitarknoxville.com

Brazieros
6901 Kingston Pike, 865-247-0295
brazeiros.com

Taqueria La Herradura
2625 N Broadway, 865-951-1170
taquerialaherradura.business.site

Gosh Ethiopian Restaurant
3609 Sutherland Ave., 865-544-4475
goshethiopian.net

7

HAVE A NICE DAY
AT THE NICEST PLACE IN AMERICA

While perhaps not as lengthy as Petro's history, Yassin's Falafel House has its own story to tell. Yassin Terou, a refugee from Syria, came to Knoxville in 2011. His relationship with a local mosque was symbiotic, relying on fellow members for food and clothing while selling sandwiches after prayers. In 2014, he opened a place downtown, welcoming people with a rainbow-colored sign stating, "All sizes, all colors, all ages, all sexes, all cultures, all religions, all types, all beliefs, all people, safe here at Yassin's Falafel House." In 2018, the restaurant was recognized by *Reader's Digest* and ABC's *Good Morning America* as the "Nicest Place in America." Yassin works day and night to help people in need in Knoxville and beyond. He's a beacon of light to the Knoxville community and an inspiration for us all in the pursuit of the American dream.

706 Walnut St., 865-219-1462
159 N Peters Rd., 865-247-7567
yassinsfalafelhouse.com

TIP

My go-to order is a "chicken shawarma, regular, light garlic," and I confess to eating it at an absurd frequency. In addition to my fave, you'll find homemade tahini and hummus, gyros, and the namesake falafel.

8

TRAVERSE
THE ALE TRAIL

The craft beer scene in Knoxville continues to expand, but it can be hard to choose the right brewery to suit one's taste. Solve this by starting your Ale Trail journey at Knox Brew Hub. Bartenders turned concierge, they'll help find the perfect brew for you. Like European ales? They might recommend Schulz Bräu, a German castle with a lovely biergarten. Digging sours? A trip to the Oak Room by Abridged is in store. Interested in something unique to Knoxville? Walk to the Old City for what is possibly the only place in the world where you can drink beer in handblown glasses and watch both artistic processes on-site at Pretentious Beer & Glass Co. Looking for a lesson with your lager? Book a guided three-hour, four-brewery tour with Knox Brew Tours (yep, same cool people as the Hub). You'll get a behind-the-scenes look at the brewing process from grain to glass and an introduction to each brewery's unique history, all while tasting 12 different styles of beer.

TIP

Pick up an Ale Trail passport at the Visit Knoxville Visitors Center, or download a digital passport for a complete list of breweries to explore. visitknoxville.com/aletrail

BREWERIES ON THE ALE TRAIL

Downtown

Balter Beerworks
Pretentious Beer Co.
Downtown Grill & Brewery

Downtown/East

Last Days of Autumn Brewing

Downtown/North

Barrelhouse by Gypsy Circus Cider
Crafty Bastard Brewery
Geezers Brewery
Next Level Brewing Company
Schulz Bräu Brewing Company
Xül Beer Company
Yee-Haw Brewing Co.

North

The Oak Room by Abridged
Elst Brewing Company
Fanatic Brewing Company
Hexagon Brewing Company
Ebony & Ivory Brewing

South

Alliance Brewing Company
Printshop Beer Co.

West

Abridged Beer Company
Albright Grove Brewing Company
Orange Hat Brewing Co.
Smoky Mountain Brewery

9

CATCH A SKYLINE SUNSET
FROM A ROOFTOP BAR

From glitzy to scruffy, you have several options for watching the setting sun. The Five Thirty Lounge atop the Hyatt Place (home of the former Historic Farragut Hotel) offers stunning views of the Smoky Mountains from 10 stories up. Across the street is the Embassy Suites, with the Radius Rooftop Lounge crowning the 14th floor and providing a nearly 360-degree view. Preservation Pub in Market Square is a swift departure in vibe from these glam hotel bars. It's Knoxville's longest-running rooftop bar whose owners have played a big role in revitalizing historic buildings (hence, "Preservation" Pub). Expect 300-plus beers on three floors, with the crest consisting of the Magic Beer Tree with kitschy plastic flamingos for company. Live music, regulars, and shenanigans are abundant. Flanking the pub's opposite side, Bernadette's Crystal Gardens is an artists' showcase with four stories of lounges surrounded by 94 million carats of crystals, gems, and fossils. Scruffy City Hall sidles the pub with a gothic twist, ideal for intimate shows and people-watching above the square.

Five Thirty Lounge
530 S Gay St., 865-770-4078
fivethirtylounge.com

Radius Rooftop Lounge
507 S Gay St., 865-770-5989
radiusrooftopbar.com

Preservation Pub
28 Market Sq., 865-524-2224
scruffycity.com/preservation-pub

Bernadette's Crystal Gardens
26 Market Sq., 865-524-2224
scruffycity.com/bernadettes-crystal-gardens

Scruffy City Hall
32 Market Sq., 865-333-4533
scruffycity.com/scruffy-city-hall

10

MAKE A TOAST
TO THE TENNESSEE WHISKEY TRAIL

Knoxville has three stops on the Tennessee Whiskey Trail, the Tri-Star State's answer to our northern neighbor's Bourbon Trail: PostModern Spirits, Knox Whiskey Works, and Drop Zone Distilling. Knox Whiskey Works is the first (legal) distillery in Knoxville, established in 2015. Known for their award-winning Old City Heirloom Corn Whiskey, they produce other favorites like their Jackson Ave Gin, Marble City Pink Gin, and the perfect shade of orange Tennessee Tailgate Orange Flavored Vodka. PostModern Spirits is where artistry meets science for top-notch craft distilling. From their Giniferous Gin to their Elderberry Gin Liqueur, you'll easily be able to taste real ingredients and botanicals. Both PostModern and KWW distribute to restaurants and bars acros East Tennessee, or you can take a bottle home from the source—both websites list cocktail recipes to enjoy your new purchases at home. Drop Zone Distilling is a military and law enforcement–themed distillery, with recipes dating back to the owner's great grandfather. Legal moonshine is available in several flavors to savor, alongside whiskey, rum, and vodka.

PostModern Spirits
205 W Jackson Ave., 865-437-3190
postmodernspirits.com

Knox Whiskey Works
516 W Jackson Ave., 865-525-2372
knoxwhiskeyworks.com/home

Drop Zone Distilling
806 E Governor John Sevier Hwy., 865-219-3219
drinkdropzone.com

11

SCREAM FOR ICE CREAM
AT THE PHOENIX PHARMACY AND CRUZE FARM

Did you know there's a word for the nostalgia one feels for a place that was before your time? That word is "anemoia," and it's the best way to describe the experience at the Phoenix Pharmacy & Fountain. A step into the circa 1899 building takes visitors past the poodle skirts and vinyl booths of the fifties into a 1930s-era-neighborhood authentic soda fountain and working pharmacy. Expect to have some of the best premium small-batch ice cream and toppings (like marshmallow fluff!), all made in-house.

In a different direction, Cruze Farm Ice Cream features "dairy girls" clad in iconic red-and-white gingham swirling farm-fresh ice cream. Service with a cherry-red smile, you can enjoy soft-serve cones at their downtown location or in East Knoxville at the Asbury House. You'll see their passion in their motto, "Work hard, love harder!"

The Phoenix Pharmacy & Fountain
418 S Gay St., 865-692-1603
thephoenixpharmacyknoxville.com

Cruze Farm Ice Cream & Dairy
445 S Gay St., Ste. 103, 865-333-1265
2721 Asbury Rd., 865-333-1265
cruzefarm.com

FILL YOUR TOTE BAG
AT THE MARKET SQUARE FARMERS MARKET

Whether you're looking for weekly provisions or just to enjoy the conviviality of a summer Saturday downtown, everyone loves the Market Square Farmers Market (MSFM for short). A part of Nourish Knoxville, the MSFM is a producer-only market, meaning all items are made or grown by the vendors. While Saturdays feature a larger setup with an extensive array of fresh veggies, handcrafted items, and other booths, the Wednesday markets are just as good for a gander. The holiday markets in December are especially joyful, and a limited winter market carries us through until spring is welcomed with open arms.

865-805-8687
nourishknoxville.org/market-square-farmers-market

13

EAT YOUR WAY THROUGH KNOXVILLE ON A FOOD TOUR

A great way to nosh here and there is by joining Knoxville Food Tours for an afternoon of history, food, and fun. Examples of stops include Chivo Taqueria, Myrtle's Chicken & Beer, Southern Grit, Fin Two Japanese Ale House, Good Golly Tamale, and more. Expect about a mile walking tour of the downtown area with guide and author Paula Johnson for about 2.5 to 3 hours. Driving tours of Bearden and Old North Knoxville are also available. Tours run year-round and vendors, samplings, and tastings change through the seasons. Tour attendees are also provided with coupons to various local attractions and shops.

knoxvillefoodtours.com

SIP IN A SWING
AT K BREW

Like Knoxville's beer scene, the coffee scene has a lot to offer. If you only had time for one shop, it might have to be K Brew on Broadway. Inside this redeveloped Texaco station, enjoy house-roasted beans while you swing in their unique hammock seating. Be sure to snap a selfie at the Greetings from Knoxville mural on the adjacent building. Add a few more shops to try with Wild Love Bakehouse, named "Best Bakery in the US" by *AFAR Magazine* in 2017 (try a hand tart or galette). Get caffeinated at Honeybee Coffee in SoKno before heading off for Urban Wilderness adventures with ethically sourced, locally roasted, and locally brewed coffee. If you find yourself on the University of Tennessee campus, Capybara Coffee is a must—the owners are from Brazil and passionate about Brazilian coffee culture. The Golden Roast is another locally roasted option, and their cozy place on Sutherland is a sure spot to rub elbows with locals surrounded by plants and local art.

K Brew
1138 N Broadway, 865-448-7498
knoxvillebrew.com

Wild Love Bakehouse
1625 N Central St., 865-200-8078
wildlovebakehouse.com

Honeybee Coffee
700 Sevier Ave., 865-200-5799
honeybeecoffeeco.com

Capybara Coffee
2457 University Commons Way, 865-851-9540
capybaracoffee.com

The Golden Roast
2250 Sutherland Ave., Ste. 125, 865-247-7704
tgroast.com

DUST OFF YOUR SPURS
AT LONESOME DOVE

Celebrity chef and UT (Tennessee, that is, not Texas) grad Tim Love combines urban and western in this Old City gem. A fine-dining experience awaits in the historic Patrick Sullivan Saloon building, called one of the best surviving examples of a downtown saloon in the southeastern United States according to Knox Heritage. At the modern Lonesome Dove Western Bistro, diners savor bold flavors, wild game, and other menu items featuring Chef Love's signature wood-fired cooking techniques. Plan on several courses, starting with the Wild Game Fettine. Relish in their cloche-smoked bourbon to accompany your rabbit-rattlesnake sausage or antelope short rib.

100 N Central St., 865-999-5251
lonesomedoveknoxville.com

LAY DOWN THE LAW
AT SALOON 16

UT great Peyton Manning needs no introduction, but for the sports-challenged, he finished his illustrious college career holding an incredible 42 NCAA, SEC, and Tennessee records. He was unsurprisingly the number one draft pick in the 1998 NFL Draft by the Indianapolis Colts, winning two Super Bowls during his Hall of Fame career of 18 years in the NFL. You could say we're kind of big fans of "the Sheriff" around here. Whether you're in town on game day or just a weekday, a visit to Saloon 16 is a must. This western-inspired, high-end watering hole at the Graduate Knoxville is filled with Manning memorabilia, and the Sheriff himself sometimes strolls through the swinging doors. Enjoy their perfectly themed menu with items such as Pat Summitt's Royal Sprite and John Ward's Loaded Cheese Fries.

1706 Cumberland Ave., 865-437-5500
graduatehotels.com/knoxville/restaurant/saloon-16

TIP

True University of Tennessee fans should make time to explore the lobby of the Graduate—it's chock-full of all kinds of UT memorabilia. Don't forget to check out the side of the Graduate too for an incredible mural that pays homage to Peyton, Neyland Stadium, and all things Vol orange.

LIFT YOUR PINKY
AT THE TENNESSEAN

From high noon (at Saloon 16) to high tea, THE TENNESSEAN Personal Luxury Hotel serves up swank in the Drawing Room. Enjoy their bridal tea before the big day, or plan for a specialty tea date such as Mother's Day. Sip on their signature Sweet Peach Noir tea that is sure to transport you through time. Nibble delicate scones and tea sandwiches as you marvel the unique view of the neighboring Sunsphere. The tea service menu is well balanced with both sweet and savory items, guaranteed to please the palette. For those who are celebrating the bride, toast the happy couple with champagne service and an amuse-bouche course with wedding colors represented in the tiered courses.

531 Henley St., 865-232-1800
thetennesseanhotel.com/dining

TIP

Take your tea to the next level with an overnight stay at THE TENNESSEAN. These luxury Tennessee River–themed suites are sure to delight both visitors and locals looking for a staycation.

CONSUME COCKTAILS
IN CONCEALMENT

Don't call us, we'll call you—and we probably won't do that because we have no cell reception. Why? Because we're literally in a bank vault underground! The Vault is a vibrant below-ground lounge in the historic Holston Bank Building, beneath the pan-Latin restaurant Vida. Think old Hollywood, *The Great Gatsby*, and all the glam of the roaring twenties. While we're on the subject, what is more twenties than a speakeasy? You'll find it (or maybe you won't) at the Peter Kern Library. Once you've gained entry—look in the alley for a red light . . . and be sure you know the password—you'll enjoy some of the most well-crafted cocktails around.

The Vault
531 S Gay St., 865-544-8564
thevaultknoxville.com

Peter Kern Library
407 Union Ave., 865-521-0050
theoliverhotel.com/peter-kern-library

19

GO FORTH, GO NORTH
IN NORTH KNOXVILLE

A major north–south thoroughfare, Broadway runs through all of North Knoxville. Enjoy breakfast at Rami's Cafe, Blossom Bowls, or The Donut Shop. Bagel-and-coffee types should pick Paysan and next-door Remedy Coffee. For an odd excursion, with brew in hand, walk across to Old Gray Cemetery, the final resting place for the who's who of Knoxville's past in a historic Victorian graveyard. Continue your adventure at Sharp's Ridge Veteran's Memorial Park, a hiking and mountain-biking favorite. Shop nearby at Lost & Found Records, Pop Weasel Emporium, and Oglewood Avenue. Lunch at Jackie's Dream or Taqueria La Herradura. Follow with Instagram-worthy drinks at Tonya Rea's Teas. Then sample different brews; North Knoxville is home to a quarter of the breweries on Knoxville's Ale Trail, and several are walkable: Xül, Geezers, Crafty Bastard, Next Level, and Gypsy Circus Barrelhouse, which is one of only five wild cider barrelhouses in the United States focusing on lambics and other wild strains of cider. End with Ale' Rae's Gastropub with live music, or A Dopo, a wood-fired pizzeria specializing in sourdough Neapolitan-style pies.

Rami's Cafe
3553 N Broadway, 865-801-9067
ramiscafe.com/menu

Blossom Bowls
1324 N Broadway, 865-333-5524
blossombowls.com

The Donut Shop
724 N Broadway, 865-816-4361
facebook.com/thedonutshopknox

Paysan Bread & Bagels
804 Tyson St., 865-394-9840
paysanbread.com

Remedy Coffee
800 Tyson St., 865-335-0967
remedycoffee.square.site

Old Gray Cemetery
543 N Broadway, 865-522-1424
oldgraycemetery.org

Sharp's Ridge Veteran's Memorial Park
329 Sharp's Ridge Memorial Dr.
865-215-4311
knoxvilletn.gov/government/city_departments_offices/parks_and_recreation/parks/sharp_s_ridge_veterans_memorial_park

Lost & Found Records
3710 N Broadway, 865-687-5556
facebook.com/lostandfoundrecords

Pop Weasel Emporium
611 N Gay St., 865-347-4670
facebook.com/loveumake

Jackie's Dream
1008 E Woodland Ave.
865-219-5789
jackiesdreamknoxville.com/menu

Taqueria La Herradura
2625 N Broadway, 865-951-1170
taquerialaherradura.business.site

Tonya Rea's Teas & Remedies
1328 Buchanan Ave., 865-357-5879
tonyareas.com

Xül Beer Company
213 E 5th Ave., 865-200-5119
xulbeer.com

Geezers Brewery
225 E 5th Ave., 865-213-2084
geezersbrewerytn.com

Crafty Bastard Brewery
6 Emory Pl., 865-333-4760
craftybastardbrewery.com

Next Level Brewing Company
700 N Broadway, 865-381-2114
nextlevelknox.com

Barrelhouse by Gypsy Circus
621 Lamar St.
gypsycircuscider.com

Ale' Rae's Gastropub
937 N Broadway, 865-924-2426
aleraes.live

A Dopo
516 Williams St., 865-321-1297
adopopizza.com

Oglewood Avenue
3524 N Broadway, 865-888-6719
oglewoodavenue.com

20

SURF THE SOUTH COAST
IN SOUTH KNOXVILLE

South Knoxville (aka SoKno) is such a fun area of Knoxville to explore. If you like the outdoors, beer, and chill vibes—this is the Knoxville neighborhood for you! Caffeine awaits in this area to start your day from Honeybee Coffee, CommonPlace Coffee, and South Press. Grab lunch at the appropriately named SoKno Taco. For the beer, try Printshop Beer Co., Alliance Brewing Company, and Asheville's Hi-Wire Brewing Taproom. Dinner rolls around with more choices to make: Simpl. or Redbud Kitchen (both farm to table), the Landing House (Cambodian), or South Coast Pizza (no shirt, no shoes, no problem).

Honeybee Coffee
700 Sevier Ave., 865-200-5799
honeybeecoffeeco.com

CommonPlace Coffee + Community
6000 Chapman Hwy., 865-347-2177
commonplaceknox.com

South Press
3615 Chapman Hwy., 865-900-1144
facebook.com/southpressknoxville

SoKno Taco
3701 Sevierville Pike, 865-851-8882
soknota.co

Printshop Beer Co.
1532 Island Home Ave., 865-474-9591
printshopbeer.co

Alliance Brewing Company
1130 Sevier Ave., 865-247-5355
alliancebrewing.com

Hi-Wire Brewing Taproom
2020 Barber St., 865-935-9395
hiwirebrewing.com/knoxville

Simpl.
1120 Sevier Ave., 865-474-1405
simplonsevier.com

Redbud Kitchen
906 Sevier Ave., 865-474-9277
redbudkitchen.com

Landing House
1147 Sevier Ave., 865-249-7424
landinghouse-109226.square.site

South Coast Pizza
1103 Sevier Ave., 865-200-5818
southcoastpizza.com

WATCH THE PROCESS
AT PRETENTIOUS CRAFT CO.

Possibly the only place in the world where you can enjoy a handcrafted beer in a handcrafted glass and watch the whole process from beginning to end is in Knoxville! Matthew Cummings is a glass artist and brewer, who noticed a problem in plain sight—no unique glasses for craft beer. Thus, Pretentious Glass Co. was born as a glassblowing studio dedicated to glassware designed for beer, wine, and whiskey too. Next door to the "glass side" is the "beer side," Pretentious Beer Co., which focuses on experimental and one-of-a-kind brews. You may never have the same exact beer twice! Enjoy the beer garden out back or grab a pint (or nonalcoholic soda) and head to the glass side to watch new pieces birthed from the ovens.

Pretentious Glass Co.
133 S Central St., 865-249-8677
pretentiousglassco.com

Pretentious Beer Co.
131 S Central St., 865-851-7693
pretentiousbeerco.com

TIP

Impressed with the glasses and want to see something larger? Head to the University of Tennessee for an enormous sculpture of handmade glass flames that come together to form a large torch and hangs near the entrance of the Student Union.

22

TASTE TENNESSEE
AT TSALI NOTCH WINERY

After sharing so much incredible beer, it only seemed fair to include a winery. Head an hour southwest of Knoxville to Madisonville, to the foothills where you'll find a beautiful vineyard and tasting room at Tsali Notch. They specialize in a specific grape variety—the muscadine—which is indigenous to the southeastern United States, and this unique style of wine is not found in too many other places. Enjoy tasting six different varieties as you bask in the mountain landscapes. During harvest season, you can even pick your own muscadines for juice, jelly, or wine-making. If you can't get enough, subscribe to their Truly Muscadine Club for hand-selected March/July/November bottles delivered to your door!

162 Harrison Rd., Madisonville, TN, 423-506-9895
tsalinotch.com

TIP

This winery is close to the Cherohala Skyway, a 43-mile National Scenic Byway that takes you from Tellico Plains, Tennessee, to Robbinsville, North Carolina. Views on views!

Bijou Theatre. Courtesy of Visit Knoxville

MUSIC AND ENTERTAINMENT

GIVE REGARDS TO BROADWAY
AT THE TENNESSEE THEATRE

A trip to Knoxville simply wouldn't be complete without experiencing a performance inside the Official State Theatre of Tennessee. Opened in 1928, this stunningly opulent "movie palace" in a Spanish-Moorish design style has a 90-plus-year year history from a single-screen movie theater to multiuse programming, including classical music, vintage films, dance, Broadway, and stellar performances by today's hottest musicians and yesterday's favorites. Local arts organizations such as the Knoxville Symphony Orchestra, Knoxville Opera, and others use the Tennessee Theatre throughout the year. Broadway enthusiasts who consider season tickets will be rewarded with a series of six shows over a half-year time frame. Perfect for date night!

604 S Gay St., 865-684-1200
tennesseetheatre.com

TIP

If you're in Knoxville on the first Monday of the month, you're lucky enough to attend Mighty Musical Monday, a free concert performance featuring the Mighty Wurlitzer organ. The Wurlitzer at the Tennessee Theatre is one of the few theater organs installed in its original location. The organ is also played prior to each Summer Movie Magic presentation.

SHINE BRIGHT
AT THE BIJOU THEATRE

While smaller than the Tennessee Theatre, the Bijou Theatre has no shortage of history. It was originally built in 1817 as the Lamar House, and from hotel to Civil War hospital, the property saw a lot of action. The original Lamar House building would continue to operate as hotel, store, and restaurant, and the theater itself opened in 1909. Vaudeville was a mainstay before motion pictures. In 1965, the lease ended, becoming an "adult" movie house with a name change to the Bijou Art Theatre. In 1971, the Lamar House was bequeathed to Church Street United Methodist Church, and unhappy about owning the once ill-reputed house, the church quickly sold it. A closure followed in 1975, and the building was scheduled for demolition. A series of fundraisers brought the theater back to life to shine like a gem in Knoxville's crown. Today, visitors can experience the Knoxville Jazz Orchestra, Chamber Classics of the Knoxville Symphony Orchestra, comedians, concerts, and more performances.

803 S Gay St., 865-522-0832
knoxbijou.org

GET DOWN
AT THE CLARENCE BROWN THEATRE

The Clarence Brown Theatre (CBT) is on the campus of the University of Tennessee and is a member of the League of Resident Theatres (LORT). With 72 member theaters, 12 of those being academic theaters, LORT is the largest professional theater association of its kind in the United States. This allows the CBT—named after legendary filmmaker and 1910 alumnus of the University of Tennessee—to bring professional talent for all to enjoy. In conjunction with the Department of Theatre at UT, the CBT provides quality programs of study at both the undergraduate and graduate level for students pursuing careers in theater. Various performances are held throughout the academic calendar.

1714 Andy Holt Ave., 865-974-5161
clarencebrowntheatre.com

TIP

If theater is really your jam, plan to attend a show with a "Talk Back" for an informal experience with cast and crew, or join for select Sunday performances to go behind the scenes.

BREAK A LEG
AT THE KNOXVILLE CHILDREN'S THEATRE

Hosting a new performance almost monthly, the Knoxville Children's Theatre is a powerhouse in the community and the Southeast's preeminent theater for children by children. Believing that theatrical arts are for everyone, Knoxville Children's Theatre has established a diverse organization where any child can participate in a production at no cost. Their impressive lineup features modified Shakespeare greats, junior versions of Disney favorites, and a wide range of other performances. Auditions are held prior to each production, allowing opportunity for new actors to test their skills and returning enthusiasts to be cast into more prominent roles. Treat the whole family to a show and encourage a lifelong love for the performing arts!

109 E Churchwell Ave., 865-208-3677
knoxvillechildrenstheatre.com

27

DANCE A JIG
AT BOYD'S JIG AND REEL

Knoxville has a strong history of Scottish culture, and nowhere is that more evident than at Boyd's Jig and Reel. A place for musicians and whisky lovers alike, it's a hot spot in the Old City to celebrate the heritage of the Scots Irish immigrants who settled in East Tennessee. They aim to represent nearly every distillery in Scotland, and their extensive whisky collection is one of the largest in the world. With more than 950 varieties, you could sample one daily for two and a half years straight and not have the same one twice! During a tasting, be sure to stick around for the Scottish and Irish music. Bring your fiddle, pick up a tuned instrument ready to play, or just sit back and enjoy the sounds of Appalachia with traditional Scottish fare, including fish-and-chips, shepherd's pie, or bangers and mash.

101 S Central St., 865-247-7066
jigandreel.com

HOOT 'N' HOLLER
AT THE WDVX BLUE PLATE SPECIAL

The WDVX Blue Plate Special® is a live radio program held at noon. Mondays through Thursdays and Saturdays are hosted at the WDVX studios at Visit Knoxville, and Fridays are hosted at Barley's Taproom and Pizzeria in the Old City for "The Big Plate." Host Red Hickey starts these performances with "Hey y'all, welcome to the Blue Plate Special!" and your practice round to clap and cheer throughout the show! The show is an hour long, typically with two sets. Music ranges from blues to bluegrass, country to Celtic, folk to funk, rockabilly to hillbilly, and more, and you truly never know who you might find on stage.

301 S Gay St., 865-544-1029
wdvx.com/program/blue-plate-special

TIP

Catch another live show on First Fridays with WDVX's Taps & Tunes with host Evie Andrus. The program starts at 6 p.m. at Visit Knoxville and features a monthly musical guest or maker, and host Evie Andrus is sure to entertain with some fiddlin'!

SEE A SHOW
AT THE THEATRE KNOXVILLE DOWNTOWN

The Theatre Knoxville Downtown has been producing community theater in Knoxville since 1976. Patrons can expect an intimate environment in a renovated church, giving opportunity for close-up action. By intimate environment, I mean sitting close enough to see stage makeup—it's such a treat to witness! Several shows are produced annually, with a wide range of comedies and dramas, classic stage versions of Hitchcock films or Agatha Christie mysteries, rom-coms, and all kinds of other productions. Christmastime is especially fun with an annually selected holiday piece that typically has the audience splitting their stockings with laughter. You're sure to feel their passion in making great theater possible!

800 S Central St., 865-544-1999
theatreknoxville.com

UNITE IN STORYTELLING
AT THE RIVER & RAIL THEATRE

A look at a map of downtown Knoxville shows rough borders of the Tennessee River to the south and the railroad lines to the north. Historically, these two elements of transportation have aided in Knoxville's growth, as well as caused separation in terms of demographics and life experiences in the city. "The goal of River & Rail Theatre is to not just create professional theatre accessible to all Knoxvillians, but to create theatre true to the stories of Knoxville, shared collectively by those on every side of every line." Patrons can expect a curated season full of laughter, tears, and deep conversations long after the curtain is closed. Performances take place at the Old City Performing Arts Center (OCPAC).

111 State St., 865-310-2664
riverandrailtheatre.com

ROCK OUT
AT THE SCHOOL OF MUSIC

The School of Music is a department within the College of Arts and Sciences at the University of Tennessee, providing a broad and comprehensive professional music program. They offer more than 200 performances and events annually, and the vast majority are free and open to the public. There are three performance halls on campus where these take place: the Sandra G. Powell Recital Hall in the Natalie L. Haslam Music Center located at 1741 Volunteer Boulevard, and the James R. Cox Auditorium and Performance Hall 32, both in the Alumni Memorial Building located at 1408 Middle Drive. Check their calendar to enjoy recitals, ensembles, and other performances by students and guest musicians from all over the world.

117 Natalie L. Haslam Music Center, 1741 Volunteer Blvd., 865-974-3241
music.utk.edu

32

FIDDLE AROUND
ON THE CRADLE OF COUNTRY MUSIC TOUR

Everyone knows Nashville as "Music City" where, today, country music rules the roost. Many fans know Bristol as the "Birthplace of Country Music" where the genre's roots were established based on the 1927 Bristol Sessions. But many don't know that Knoxville was instrumental (pun intended) in the development of country music. Take a stroll on the self-guided Cradle of Country Music Tour to learn about Knoxville's ties to Hank Williams, Elvis Presley, Dolly Parton, the Everly Brothers, Roy Acuff, and others. Pick up a brochure at the Knoxville Visitors Center to begin your journey back in time.

visitknoxville.com/things-to-do/tours/guided

TIP

Prefer an audio guide? The Knoxville History Project has a paid option through the VoiceMap app. After downloading "Knoxville Legends: Exploring the City's Country Music Heritage," explore 24 stops in this version with tidbits along the way voiced by KHP's executive director, Jack Neely.

TUNE INTO
THE KNOXVILLE SYMPHONY ORCHESTRA

Exciting . . . elegant . . . entertaining . . . all describe the Knoxville Symphony Orchestra (KSO), a powerhouse in the Knoxville community and the oldest continuously performing symphony orchestra in the Southeast. To the novice, their calendar may seem daunting, but after a quick study, it's easy to understand their diverse programming. Masterworks concerts are typically held at the Tennessee Theatre—the demonstration of classics such as Beethoven and Dvořák performed by the KSO. Similarly, the Chamber Classic Series is presented in the more intimate Bijou Theatre. Pops Concerts brings a modern twist to the symphony with music from film, Broadway, and popular music. The Q series features one-hour lunchtime concerts by the Principal Woodwind Quintet and the Principal String Quartet. As KSO founder Bertha Walburn Clark said, "Every important occasion in life must have music."

knoxvillesymphony.com

TIP

Don't miss KSO on the Road—free, family-friendly concerts in various locations, including Symphony on the Square in Market Square, Festival on the Fourth in World's Fair Park, and elsewhere such as the Knoxville Botanical Garden and Arboretum.

34

UNPACK YOUR BAGS
AT THE CARPETBAG THEATRE

From stage performances to theater festivals to youth camps to open-mic nights to spoken-word poetry, the Carpetbag Theatre has been producing original theatrical works for more than 50 years in Knoxville. Their mission, per their website, is to "give artistic voice to the issues and dreams of people who have been silenced by racism, classism, sexism, ageism, homophobia and other forms of oppression," and their ensemble achieves that goal through their varied productions. Get to know this organization and check out their events calendar for the next performance that is sure to help you appreciate the range of our collective experiences.

1323 N Broadway, 865-544-0447
carpetbagtheatre.org

35

C'MON GET HAPPY
IN CENTRAL/HAPPY HOLLER

If a neighborhood name like "Happy Holler" doesn't drive you to explore, I don't know what would. Central is a north–south route in North Knoxville running parallel-ish to Broadway. In addition to great food, brews, and vintage shopping in this area, there are lots of places to track down entertainment. Got kids? Choose the Knoxville Children's Theatre—expect a professional production for children, by children. You'll find the junior version of Disney favorites, mysteries, and maybe even modified Shakespeare. All ages can enjoy Central Cinema, a neighborhood movie house featuring cult classics and staff favorites. Viewers will find first-run independent films, local-interest films, and the occasional live comedy. Check out their regular series, and dedicated theme nights such as kung fu, anime, and more. For an LGBTQ+ friendly atmosphere, Club XYZ dubs itself "Knoxville's Friendliest Gay Place to Be." The nightclub hosts drag nights, bingo, karaoke, and a solid calendar of other performances and events.

LISTEN UP
AT BIG EARS

The Big Ears Festival has got to be one of the more unique music festivals I've ever experienced. The artists and their music are carefully curated, eclectic, global, ethereal, and profound. The performances and their venues are just as varied, from historic theaters such as the Tennessee and the Bijou, to intimate galleries and acoustically perfect churches. The festival organizers do an incredible job of pairing those performances with appropriate venues, making fitting choices like hosting delicate string quartets inside St. John Episcopal Cathedral, and providing funky jazz ensembles with the space and freedom to blast away at the Mill & Mine. They're all within walking distance, seemingly designed to make no two festivalgoers' experience the same.

bigearsfestival.org

TIP

Dedicate your weekend to the event, and plan ahead. I typically listen to two to three songs from each artist scheduled to perform in the weeks leading up to the festival to narrow down what I can realistically attend and personally enjoy.

OPEN UP TO THE OPERA
AT THE ROSSINI FESTIVAL

Music lovers, particularly those of opera, will love the Rossini Festival International Street Fair that takes place in Knoxville every spring. This signature program of the Knoxville Opera includes multiple stages with hours of entertainment by hundreds of artists. Expect to see downtown Knoxville's streets turn into a street fair of epic proportions! Stroll your way through artisan and food vendors as you listen to arias. You'll feel like you've been transported to Florence during the Renaissance period, but with modern amenities such as cell phone service to post photos of gigantic and delicious roasted turkey legs. Huzzah!

knoxvilleopera.com/rossini

BE MERRY AND GO ROUND

AT THE TENNESSEE VALLEY FAIR

The Tennessee Valley Fair is exactly what it sounds like—fairgrounds full of rides, live music, agriculture, competitions, art shows, and, of course, anything that can be fried will be fried! Corn dogs, Oreos, and funnel cake—here I come! East Tennessee has a long history of agriculture, and this annual event in September is a great way to have fun while learning about farming, animals, and more. The southwestern corner of the fair is for the kiddies; expect smaller rides and just the right amount of excitement. Larger rides are farther back, and all the lemonade, turkey legs, and other delightful things-on-a-stick are spread throughout. Established in 1916, the fair has been at Chilhowee Park for more than 100 years, and we've been having cotton candy dreams ever since!

tnvalleyfair.org

TIP

Check out their concert calendar; be sure to note it's a separate ticket from the fair itself!

Paddleboarding the Tennessee River
with Knoxville Adventure Collective.
Courtesy of Sarah Mcaffry Photography

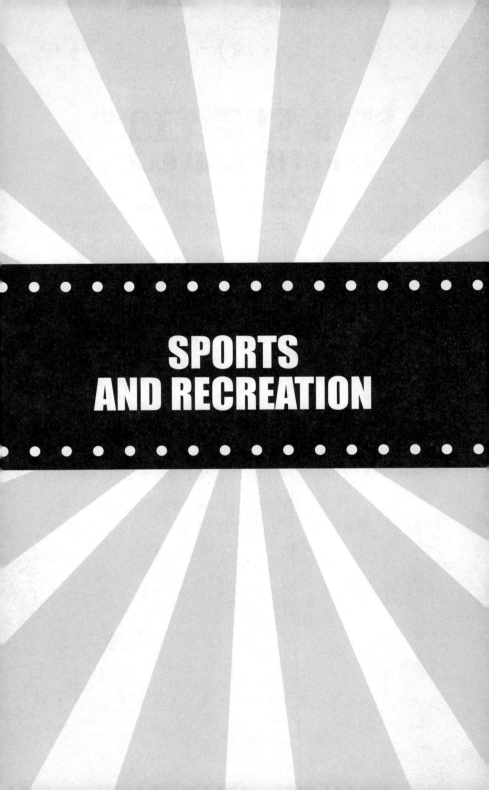

SPORTS AND RECREATION

SING "ROCKY TOP"
AT A UT FOOTBALL GAME

A fall Saturday in Knoxville would simply be incomplete without attending a University of Tennessee football game. The best thing to do is resign yourself to the day and start tailgating—or "sailgating" if you've got access to a boat (UT is one of only two universities in the United States with a stadium on the water). Make friends in Circle Park or G10 garage, and you'll be sure to have your fill of all types of goodness in no time. Be sure to stake out a spot on Peyton Manning Pass two hours before game time for the Vol Walk, where you can catch high fives from parading players along the way. Once you've made it inside to Neyland Stadium, enjoy the sounds of the Pride of the Southland marching band, as the team runs through the "Power T." Inhale the crisp fall air as you sing "Rocky Top" at the top of your lungs with the crowd. One thing's for sure: it's football time in Tennessee!

1235 Phillip Fulmer Way, 800-332-VOLS
utsports.com/sports/football

HEAD INTO
THE URBAN WILDERNESS

Just minutes from downtown across the Tennessee River is Knoxville's Urban Wilderness (KUW), a spectacular outdoor adventure area where you can hike, bike, climb, paddle, or just wander in the woods. Not a singular destination, KUW stretches across 1,000 acres of various parks, a beautiful nature center, historic sites, dramatic quarries, adventure playgrounds, and more than 50 miles of trails and greenways spread throughout. It's hard for me to pick a personal favorite—I love the serene paved trail at High Ground Park, or the unpaved paths at Fort Dickerson and River Bluff Wildlife Area. I also enjoy bringing a picnic to Suttree Landing Park with great views of downtown—great for kids, with a nice playground. Mountain bikers will want to go to Baker Creek Preserve, which is home to the region's only double black diamond trail. Baker Creek also has pump tracks and an area where beginners can test their skills.

visitknoxville.com/urban-wilderness

41

BE ONE WITH NATURE
AT IJAMS NATURE CENTER

Hiking, biking, paddling, rock climbing, and more can all be done at Ijams Nature Center. Originally the home of Harry and Alice Yoe Ijams in the early 1900s, this crown jewel of Knoxville's Urban Wilderness offers a respite from city life—just minutes from the center of the city. Situated on more than 318 acres, all ages are welcome to enjoy this free attraction. Some of the trails are paved, making them accessible and perfect for strollers, while some are natural surface—with various difficulty levels. Ijams has lots of programming for the whole family from summer camps to movie nights to presentations of Shakespearean plays. They also rehabilitate wildlife, and visitors can say hello to various regional animal species on-site. Be sure to head down the street to Mead's Quarry at Ijams for more trails and then cool off with a swim or paddle.

2915 Island Home Ave., 865-577-4717
ijams.org

TIP

My two favorite trails are the Tower Trail to the Boardwalk, and the Imerys Trail to the Ross Quarry Marble Loop to see the Keystone. The latter is especially rocky; be sure to wear stable footwear!

GO YOUR OWN WAY
ON A GREENWAY

Walkers, runners, bikers, wheelchair users, and stroller pushers will find the perfect path on one of Knoxville's scenic paved greenways. With more than 85 miles of paved trail, enjoy natural areas in the heart of the city that follow rivers, connect to parks, and provide recreation for all kinds of outdoor enthusiasts. Several of the greenways are close to attractions such as the Urban Wilderness (Will Skelton Greenway), Mabry-Hazen House (Morningside Greenway), and Neyland Stadium (you guessed it, Neyland Greenway). The Sequoyah Hills Greenway is particularly spectacular in the spring, with dogwoods and azaleas in bloom. Knoxville Adventure Collective provides greenway bike rentals (and mountain bike and e-bike rentals too).

Knoxville Adventure Collective
900 Volunteer Landing Ln., 865-228-8424
knoxvilleadventure.com

TIP

This "Guide to Knoxville Greenways" blog post highlights several greenways with the specific attractions found along them: visitknoxville.com/blog/post/guide-to-knoxville-greenways

SHOUT "LET'S GO, ICE BEARS!"
AT A KNOXVILLE ICE BEARS HOCKEY GAME

GOOOOALLLL! What's more exhilarating than a fast-paced hockey game? See the Knoxville Ice Bears as they face off against opponents on their home ice at the Knoxville Civic Coliseum. Part of the Southern Professional Hockey League (SPHL) and four-time SPHL champions, the Ice Bears are a family-friendly way to ward off the winter doldrums. Hockey has been gaining interest in the South, particularly in Tennessee, where the NHL's Nashville Predators have seen an increasingly loyal fan base—and the sport's passion has spread to Knoxville. Check the Ice Bears calendar for themed games, which range from *Star Wars* night with lightsaber battles to the infamous Wiener Dog Races night where small but mighty dachshunds waddle to win!

500 Howard Baker Jr. Dr., 865-525-7825
knoxvilleicebears.com

44

SHOOT HOOPS
AT THE WOMEN'S BASKETBALL HALL OF FAME

Pat Summitt's incredible legacy as head coach of UT's Lady Vols played a big part in Knoxville's opportunity to be home to the Women's Basketball Hall of Fame—the only facility of its kind dedicated to all levels of women's basketball. Outside the museum, you'll see the world's largest basketball, measuring 30 feet tall and weighing 10 tons. Upon entering the aptly named Pat Summitt Rotunda, you'll see a 17-foot bronze statue exemplifying their mission to "honor the past, celebrate the present, and promote the future" of women's basketball. During the annual induction into the Hall of Fame, each inductee receives a replica of this statue. Enjoy learning about the sport and iconic athletes and coaches throughout history. Be sure to save your energy for the lower level where you can test your skills on three different courts, a dribbling course, and a passing skills area!

700 Hall of Fame Dr., 865-633-9000
wbhof.com

TELL A SECRET
AT THE KNOXVILLE BOTANICAL GARDEN

Can you keep a secret? This one should be shared! The Knoxville Botanical Garden and Arboretum is a 47-acre public garden located in East Knoxville, just two miles from downtown. The history of the former Howell Nursery spans more than 200 years, and today the KBGA has a number of garden displays, unique plant specimens, extensive stone walls and architecture, and an impressive dogwood collection. There is an actual "secret garden" on-site, and it's certainly worth a stroll to find. Although there's no reference to the property, it's a fun literary connection to author Frances Hodgson Burnett—the English author who wrote *The Secret Garden* in 1911 and surprisingly lived in Knoxville just after the Civil War. Add this one to your "free things to do" list and visit the garden anytime; they're open 365 days a year from dawn to dusk.

Note: Due to the varying terrain with gravel and mulch paths, KBGA is not currently accessible to those with limited mobility. Pets welcome on leash.

2743 Wimpole Ave., 865-862-8717
knoxgarden.org

TIP

Though spring when the dogwoods are flowering might be hard to beat, the garden is beautiful year-round. Check their website section "What's in Bloom" if you are looking to see a particular plant.

PACK A PICNIC
AT UT GARDENS

This nationally recognized garden is part of the University of Tennessee system and as such functions as an outdoor laboratory. Students and professional agriculturalists analyze a variety of plants and their environments to understand and demonstrate how plants can best be used in landscapes. Visitors to the UT Gardens not only enjoy the incredible variety of annuals, perennials, ornamental grasses, and aquatic plants but also get ideas for their home gardens as well. If all this sounds too technical or like you should have paid more attention in botany class, not to worry. This garden is perfect for visitors of all ages and all interest levels, and ditto to Knoxville Botanical Garden and Arboretum—free and open sunrise to sunset 365 days a year.

Note: Paths are mostly gravel and mulch. Pets welcome on leash.

2518 Jacob Dr., 865-974-7324
utgardens.tennessee.edu

CRUISE
THE TENNESSEE RIVER

If self-propelled kayaks and paddleboards aren't your thing, consider a cruise aboard a powered vessel. You've got two options: the *Tennessee Riverboat*, also known as *The Star of Knoxville*; and the *Volunteer Princess*, a luxury yacht. The *Tennessee Riverboat* is an authentic paddlewheel vessel that can accommodate 235 passengers. They have weekly lunch and dinner cruises, day and evening sightseeing cruises, and seasonal cruises. The *Volunteer Princess* is a modern and luxurious dining cruise vessel, accommodating 132 passengers. Similar to the *Tennessee Riverboat*, they have events ranging from Motown Monday to Casino Night.

Tennessee Riverboat
300 Neyland Dr., 865-525-7827
tnriverboat.com

Volunteer Princess
956 Volunteer Landing Ln., 865-247-6584
volunteerprincess.com

SPARE AN AFTERNOON
AT MAPLE HALL

This is not the suburban, smoky bowling alley of your childhood. No funky odors cling to the ancient carpet, and there's no mystery nacho cheese. Maple Hall is a spirited bowling experience, below street level downtown in the historic JC Penney Building. It only has 11 lanes, with two of those being private and four semiprivate. It's an all-age affair until 9 p.m. when it's 21 and up. Lanes are filled on a first-come, first-served basis, and Friday and Saturday evenings typically come with a bit of a wait. Not to worry—enjoy some top-shelf beverages upstairs in the Maple Room (always 21 and over). Hungry? No stale hot dogs rotating into oblivion here—you'll find Tennessee Stacks (varying options served over natural-cut fries), bacon jam burgers, and Memphis charcuterie. This is an outing sure to bowl you over!

414 S Gay St. 865-249-8454
maplehallknox.com

50

SWING THROUGH THE TREES
AT NAVITAT

Part zip-lining, part obstacle course, Navitat is the spot for anyone up for an aerial adventure. Adjacent to Ijams Nature Center in Knoxville's Urban Wilderness, this treetop park offers six adventure trails ranging from easy to difficult. Each trail consists of 8–12 "elements," which include bridges, swings, nets, climbs, zip lines, and more. It's the perfect thrill for the whole family as ages seven and up can safely navigate the course. Plan for approximately two-plus hours as they get you outfitted with safety gear, demonstrate how to "clip in" your harness to the various elements, and give you plenty of time to actually explore. They even offer Navitat at Night—an adventure under the stars and twinkling lights!

2915 Island Home Ave., 865-628-4828
navitatknoxville.com

51

ALL YOU HAVE TO DO IS DREAM

AT EVERLY BROTHERS PARK

Are you a fan of the Beatles? How about the Rolling Stones? Simon & Garfunkel? If you said yes, did you know that members from each of these groups said that the Everly Brothers inspired their sound? You might be wondering what that has to do with Knoxville. Glad you asked! Don and Phil Everly went to West High School in Bearden in the 1950s. It was in Knoxville that they began performing as a duo, played on WROL radio, met Chet Akins, and the rest is history. The pocket park is located just a mile from where Don graduated in 1953 and honors the two with inlaid stone quotes from Paul McCartney, Graham Nash, Keith Richards, and others. In 2022, the park was added to the Tennessee Music Pathways.

4635 Kingston Pike

CHOOSE AN EVENT
AT CHILHOWEE PARK

Most visitors to the park come for events like the Tennessee Valley Fair or Street Rod Nationals South, but many likely don't know how expansive it is in terms of area or history. The park covers 81 acres and includes a 57,100-square-foot exposition center, a 1910-era bandstand, a 4,500-seat amphitheater, a three-acre lake, and the home to Muse Knoxville. In 1910 and 1911, Chilhowee Park hosted the two Appalachian Expositions, and, in 1913, the park hosted the National Conservation Exposition. Several decades before, on August 8, 1863, Andrew Johnson, military governor of Tennessee and eventual president after Lincoln's assassination, freed his personal slaves. In the early 1900s, Black people were only allowed to visit Chilhowee Park one day a year, on August 8, and the day was commemorated by Black people in Tennessee as a holiday. Today, it's known as the Eighth of August and still celebrated as a Day of Emancipation in the park. Come by for a stroll or check their calendar for a full list of events.

3301 E Magnolia Ave., 865-215-1450
chilhoweepark.com

LACE UP FOR A WALK
AT LAKESHORE PARK

Lakeshore Park is a 185-acre general recreation public park located along the Tennessee River just west of downtown in Bearden. With approximately one million annual visitors, Lakeshore Park is the most visited public park in Knoxville. It's easy to see why, with extensive paved greenways, access to the Tennessee River, and beautiful Smoky Mountain views. A mecca for families, its expansive property includes numerous soccer and baseball fields, open lawns scattered throughout, and one of the best accessible playgrounds around. Be sure to check their calendar for events like the New Ground Festival and Summer Picnic.

5930 Lyons View Pike, 865-215-1722
lakeshoreparkknoxville.org

TAKE A HIKE
AT HOUSE MOUNTAIN

House Mountain is the highest point in Knox County, situated eight miles northeast of Knoxville in Corryton. Rising to an elevation of 2,064 feet above sea level, hikers can hoof the moderate-to-difficult trails for rewarding city and mountain range views. Be prepared: the paths are rocky and steep in areas, and some hikers may feel more comfortable with trekking poles in addition to some trusty hiking boots. It's typically not too crowded compared to some other hiking opportunities in the area, and it's also a great spot for bird-watching. The loop is about four miles and takes around two and a half hours to complete. Dogs are welcome but must be on leash.

9601 Hogskin Rd., Corryton
knoxcounty.org/parks/pdfs/hiking.pdf

KICK IT
AT A ONE KNOXVILLE SOCCER GAME

With their inaugural season in 2022, One Knoxville Sporting Club is already kicking Knoxville's sports scene up a notch. Beginning as members of the South Central Division in the USL League Two, they're now members of the USL League One, the top men's professional soccer league in North America. For those who want to get in the game themselves, One Knoxville also hosts adult recreational leagues. Players can stay fit and have fun in their intermediate coed 7v7, advanced coed 6v6, or pick from their various-level 11v11 options. Individuals can sign up and be placed on an existing team, so no need to worry if you're new to the area, or none of your friends play soccer. Make some new friends, head to a One Knoxville soccer game, and remember—"There's only One Knoxville!"

oneknoxsc.com

TAKE ME OUT TO THE BALL GAME

AT THE TENNESSEE SMOKIES

As the Double-A affiliate of the Chicago Cubs, going to a Tennessee Smokies game in Seymour is a "beary good time"! Knoxville has a long history of enjoying the sport of baseball, hosting minor-league teams since the late 19th century. Modern-day enthusiasts can catch the Tennessee Smokies in action throughout the summer. Family-friendly fun awaits, with fun themes and promotions like Princesses in the Park, '90s Night, and the ubiquitous UT Night. The team will soon relocate back to its Knoxville roots in a new stadium built in the Old City. Prior to the 2000 season, the team was known as the Knoxville Smokies, and upon relocation back to Knoxville, the team and its former moniker will be reunited. Play ball!

milb.com/tennessee

BE A-MAZE-D
AT MAPLE LANE FARMS

Maple Lane Farms is a working farm in Greenback (southwest of Knoxville) that is only open in the fall. Alongside tractor-pulled hay wagons, a pumpkin patch, a campfire, photo ops, and more, the main event is the corn maze. Each year, they create a gigantic maze that is the talk of the town for miles around—the oldest corn maze in the southeast! If you like it spooky, they have a haunted corn maze option in late October. They also have your decor needs in mind, selling cornstalks, mums, straw bales, and more in their barn store. Fun fact: UT's Department of Agriculture has used their fields to experiment and find solutions for agricultural issues faced by farmers, producers, and others in the industry.

1126 Maple Ln., Greenback, 865-856-3511
tnmaplelanefarms.com

58

DO IT YOUR WAY
IN THE GREAT SMOKY MOUNTAINS NATIONAL PARK

Whole books have been written about the Smokies, and while any entry here would be woefully limited, any Knoxville bucket list would be incomplete without a mention of these beautiful Appalachian Mountains. From downtown, there are multiple route options depending on the experience you're looking for: head south on Alcoa Highway through Maryville to get to Townsend, the "peaceful side of the smokies"; or head east on I-40 to exit 407 to go down through Sevierville, Pigeon Forge, and Gatlinburg for the family-focused vacationland; alternately, consider taking Chapman Highway for a more historic route. A list of must-dos would vary based on season and desired activity level, but a drive through Cade's Cove, a hike to see a waterfall (Abrams, Laurel, Rainbow, etc.), and a trip up Clingman's Dome are all iconic. So do it your way—there's no wrong way to discover this beloved national park!

nps.gov/grsm/index.htm

James White's Fort

CULTURE AND HISTORY

59

HOLD DOWN THE FORT
AT JAMES WHITE'S FORT

To get a look at turn-of-the-century life—the 18th, not the most recent one—James White's Fort is the place to go. James White came to the area in the early 1780s and became the founder of Knoxville. Thanks to his service in the Revolutionary War, he was given a land grant of 1,000 acres (in 1791, he partitioned part of this land to establish the town that would become Knoxville). Today, visitors can see his two-story log cabin, built in 1786, and learn about the frontier lifestyle through hands-on interpretation, including open-hearth cooking, blacksmithing, and spinning. You'll walk away with a healthy appreciation for all the modern amenities—especially indoor plumbing.

205 E Hill Ave., 865-525-6514
jameswhitesfort.org

TIP

Into ghost stories? Ask them to share some spooky tales about Mrs. Kennedy!

GET CONSTITUTIONAL
AT BLOUNT MANSION

Out of all the signers of the US Constitution, only one signer's home is located outside the original 13 states. And of all the signers' homes, only a handful are open to the public. One of those is Blount Mansion National Historic Landmark, home of North Carolina signer William Blount, which is kind of a big deal! William Blount, appointed by President George Washington to govern the Southwest Territory, had this home built in 1792. Just a few short years later in 1796, Blount played a major role to have the Southwest Territory admitted to the Union as Tennessee—our nation's 16th state. See the desk where the Tennessee Constitution was written and learn about how Blount's risky land speculation and conspiracy with Great Britain resulted in being the first federal official to face impeachment. End your visit with a stroll through the 18th-century-style English gardens, lovingly maintained with help from their friends at the Knoxville Garden Club.

200 W Hill Ave., 865-525-2375
blountmansion.org

TIP

When you're touring the kitchen, there's a strange (to us modern cooks) iron tool in the kitchen that looks like a taco holder. See if you can guess what it is!

HAVE A BONNY GOOD TIME
AT MARBLE SPRINGS

Elected in 1796, John Sevier was Tennessee's first governor, and Marble Springs State Historic Site was his last home and farm. He was exactly who we think of when we think of a pioneer—a farmer, trader, solider, politician, husband, and father of 18 children. He became a hero at the 1780 Battle of Kings Mountain against the British, and eventually he served six terms as the Tennessee governor. Marble Springs is named for the Tennessee pink marble quarried nearby, and the site features elements that help interpret Tennessee's early frontier history, including a period tavern, kitchen, cabin, loom house, and spring house. Visiting the grounds is free, with paid tours as an option.

1220 W Governor John Sevier Hwy., 865-573-5508
marblesprings.net

TIP

Keep your eyes peeled for Cinnamon, the unofficial mascot of Marble Springs. According to their research, he is actually related to John Sevier's cat Fred, short for Frederick Obadiah Oliver Lawrence the First!

LOOK AROUND THE RIVER BEND
AT CRESCENT BEND

A glance at a map will show how this 1834 home got its name. Caressing the curves of the Tennessee River, this stately property was built by Drury Armstrong—the Italian terraced gardens were added later. Armstrong's land holdings included an area nearby where the Battle of Armstrong's Hill took place during the Civil War and a section of woodlands to the southeast that today makes up about 10 percent of the Great Smoky Mountains National Park. Drury divided his farm between his sons, Marcelus and Robert. After Drury's death in 1856, Marcelus stayed at Crescent Bend, and Robert built Bleak House, 500 yards west. Crescent Bend farmland witnessed the assassination of Union Brigadier General William P. Sanders when he was wounded there on November 18, 1863, presumably by a Confederate sniper from the Bleak House tower. The general died the following day at the Lamar House (now the Bijou Theatre). Today, visitors can enjoy a historic home filled with decorative arts, 18th-century furniture, and a circa 1640–1820 English silver collection.

2728 Kingston Pike, 865-637-3163
crescentbend.com

THINK PINK (OR BLUE)
AT HISTORIC RAMSEY HOUSE

Known at the time as the finest home in Tennessee, the Historic Ramsey House was built in 1797 for Francis Alexander Ramsey. Visitors can admire its unique Tennessee pink marble and blue limestone construction, as well as a period-accurate decorative art collection. Notable home details include the first attached kitchen in Tennessee, a scrolled wooden staircase (a signature of the architect), and many other housewares, furniture, and even children's items. The grounds are pet-friendly and make for a beautiful stroll or picnic.

Note: due to the structural limitations of this 200-year-old home, the Ramsey House is not wheelchair accessible.

2614 Thorngrove Pike, 865-546-0745
ramseyhouse.org

TIP

Visit in the summer to watch the Emmett Machinists or the Knoxville Holstons take on their opponents in a friendly-yet-competitive game of vintage "base ball." The Tennessee Association of Vintage Base Ball brings history to life by playing America's favorite pastime using rules, equipment, costumes, and culture of the 1860s. Play ball!

AVOID A SCANDAL
AT MABRY-HAZEN HOUSE AND BETHEL CEMETERY

Built in 1858 by Joseph Mabry, three generations of the same family resided in the Italianate-style home, giving an opportune look into 130 years of Knoxville history. A staggering 2,500 original artifacts are on display, along with several stories waiting to be heard here. Visitors can learn of Civil War struggles, an infamous gunfight on Gay Street (later chronicled by Mark Twain), a scandal involving an engagement not-to-be, and many more tales of the Mabry and Hazen families. The grounds are classified as a Level I Arboretum and offer views of downtown Knoxville and the Great Smoky Mountains. The nearby Bethel Cemetery is the final resting place of 1,600 Confederate soldiers.

1711 Dandridge Ave., 865-522-8661
mabryhazen.com

TIP

Having trouble making it to Mabry-Hazen House during business hours? Join them for their "Night at the Museum" events!

FOLLOW YOUR (HE)ART

AT HISTORIC WESTWOOD

Connect with Knoxville's art history at Historic Westwood. The "youngest" of Knoxville's historic house museums, Westwood was built in 1890 as a wedding promise for John Lutz and his bride, Adelia Armstrong Lutz (granddaughter of Drury Armstrong, owner of Crescent Bend). Adelia was a talented artist and leader in the Knoxville arts community. Their impressive Queen Anne–style house features her painting studio, designed specifically for her materials and paintings. Today, visitors can enjoy a showcase of 32 of Adelia's works alongside frescoes, stately furnishings, art, and craftsmanship from other Knoxville artists from the late 19th century to the present era. In 2022, Westwood was accepted into the National Trust for Historic Preservation's prestigious Historic Artists' Homes and Studios program.

3425 Kingston Pike, 865-523-8008
historicwestwood.org

GO BACK IN TIME
AT THE EAST TENNESSEE HISTORY CENTER

The East Tennessee History Center is a great starting point for those who want to get a solid picture of both Knoxville and East Tennessee, past and present. The Museum of East Tennessee History on the first floor spans from the time of indigenous people and pioneers up to the 1982 World's Fair in their signature exhibit *Voices of the Land*. Three centuries walk visitors through the divided loyalties of the Civil War to industrial growth, women's suffrage, the hillbilly stereotype, mountain crafts, African American contributions, the beginnings of country music, the upheaval of families relocated due to a national park, TVA lakes, and the "Secret City" and Manhattan Project of World War II. The second floor houses the Knox County Archives. The third floor houses the Calvin M. McClung Historical Collection, with genealogies, manuscripts, and other records. Be sure to check their calendar for lectures, events, and other programming.

601 S Gay St., 865-215-8824
easttnhistory.org

GO BACK FURTHER IN TIME
AT THE MCCLUNG MUSEUM

The McClung Museum of Natural History & Culture is a free Smithsonian-affiliated museum with permanent and rotating exhibits on the University of Tennessee campus. You'll know you're there when you see "Monty" the Edmontosaurus welcoming you out front! Their permanent exhibits include archeology, fossils, anthropology, and art, much of it with a Tennessee focus. Their calendar lists upcoming exhibits and special events. If you have a bit more time, walk the full loop of Circle Park to see the *Torchbearer* statue. This iconic piece appropriately symbolizes knowledge, enlightenment, truth, and intellectual optimism. The *Torchbearer* represents that the darkness of ignorance can be overcome by the light of truth and reason.

1327 Circle Park Dr., 865-974-2144
mcclungmuseum.utk.edu

TIP

Park in Circle Park and tell the booth attendant you're headed to the McClung Museum, and they'll give you a free two-hour parking pass instead of the standard 45 minutes.

PRESERVE AFRICAN AMERICAN HISTORY
AT THE BECK CULTURAL EXCHANGE CENTER

The mission of Beck is to be the place where Black history and culture are preserved, nurtured, taught, and continued. This museum in East Knoxville down the street from Mabry-Hazen House is inside a home built in 1912 by the Cowans. A Black doctor, Dr. Lennon, purchased the home in 1946, becoming the first Black family to move into the area. After cross burnings and warnings from the KKK, the area changed in racial composition, especially during the 1950s as a result of urban renewal. James and Ethel Beck purchased the home in 1968, and following their deaths in 1975, the Beck Cultural Exchange Center was established. The Beck is designated by the state as a primary repository of Black history and culture in East Tennessee and presents an opportunity for visitors to learn about this history, discover genealogy, and participate in events throughout the year, including the Alex Haley Festival, Jazz at the Beck, and the Eighth of August Jubilee.

1927 Dandridge Ave., 865-524-8461
beckcenter.net

CARVE OUT AN AFTERNOON
AT CANDORO MARBLE BUILDING

One of Knoxville's nicknames is the "Marble City," and a visit to the Candoro Marble Building in South Knoxville makes it easy to see why. This Beaux Arts structure featuring Tennessee pink marble was designed by renowned architect Charles Barber in 1921. The region's history of quarrying marble goes back 200 years, with marble shipped to Washington, DC, for use in the Washington Monument in 1848. Grand Central Station in New York City, as well as the Lincoln Memorial and the National Gallery of Art in Washington, DC, feature the prized stone. Locally, Tennessee pink marble can be found at the Knoxville Museum of Art, the East Tennessee History Center, Knoxville Botanical Garden and Arboretum, and more.

The Candoro Marble Company itself was established in 1914. Tennessee marble peaked in the 1920s and 1930s, but popularity waned, and the company closed in 1982. The building was added to the National Register of Historic Places in 1996. Visitors can tour the former showroom and enjoy art exhibitions hosted through Tri-Star Arts.

4450 Candora Ave., 865-219-3074
candoromarble.org

WIG OUT
AT THE SUNSPHERE

You know you've made it when you've been referenced on *The Simpsons*. Such is the case with Knoxville's Sunsphere, mimicked as "The Wigsphere" in a 1996 episode. This skyline icon was built for the 1982 World's Fair (the theme was "Energy Turns the World," hence the Sunsphere), and is one of only two remaining structures from that fair. A trip up to the Fourth Floor Observation Deck operated by Visit Knoxville is a 100 percent must-do to enjoy a 360-degree view of the city overlooking World's Fair Park. Even on cloudy days, the beautiful Smoky Mountains can be seen to the southeast in the distance. Impress your friends with this trivia: both Seattle's Space Needle and Paris's Eiffel Tower were also built for World's Fairs (1962 and 1889, respectively)!

810 Clinch Ave., 865-314-0660
sunspheretickets.com

TIP

Want to see the world's largest Rubik's Cube? A gift from Hungary for the World's Fair, this giant puzzle can be seen inside the Knoxville Convention Center next door!

DIVIDE AND CONQUER
ON THE CIVIL WAR DRIVING TOUR

Leading up to and during the Civil War, Knoxville was a divided city in a divided state in a divided country. Loyalties to the Union and to the Confederacy tore brothers and neighbors apart. On the Divided Loyalties Driving Tour, explore the historic homes, forts, and other sites where battle lines were drawn. Several sites overlap with the Civil War Trails®, a multistate initiative dedicated to placing markers at Civil War sites. The Divided Loyalties Driving Tour includes these and other Knoxville-centric locations. Plan for a minimum of a half day just for driving and quick stops. Plan for more to visit the museums and historic sites along the way.

visitknoxville.com/listing/civil-war-driving-tour%3A-divided-loyalties/1636

72

GET YOUR STEPS IN
WITH KNOXVILLE WALKING TOURS

Exercise and entertainment, now that I can do! Laura Still is a master storyteller, and, boy, does she have a few yarns up her sleeve. Whether you're looking for an overview of Knoxville's early history, spooky ghost tales, or something more scandalous like her "Misbehaving Women" tour, you're sure to learn a lot about Knoxville from a ground-level view. She also offers tours on the Civil War, Knoxville's literary figures, and more. Most tours are about 90 minutes (the Civil War one is closer to two hours), and generally less than a mile total walking distance at a comfortable walk-and-stop pace. Tours are done in partnership with the Knoxville History Project, and a portion of the proceeds support this incredible nonprofit organization.

865-309-4522
knoxvillewalkingtours.com

73

EVENTS BELOW EARTH
AT CHEROKEE CAVERNS

It's hard to picture, but at one time this entire region was an inland sea. Earthquakes causing cracks in dolomite rock where the water drained through eventually led to a network of caves and caverns—the ground beneath much of Kentucky and Tennessee is full of geological wonder. As another place that only has select events throughout the year, Cherokee Caverns is an incredible cave attraction just minutes from the heart of the city. They host several events annually, including Christmas in July, Trick or Treat in the Cave, and Christmas in the Cave. Expect cool temps and even cooler vendors in this unique experience. Come summer, they offer family-friendly movies too. The caverns are stroller and wheelchair accessible, and parking is free.

8524 Oak Ridge Hwy., 865-275-5196
historiccherokeecaverns.com

OPEN YOUR EYES
AT THE KNOXVILLE MUSEUM OF ART

The Knoxville Museum of Art (KMA) is a FREE museum that is a great introduction to artists from and inspired by East Tennessee. Their Higher Ground exhibit is dedicated to exactly that, while their "Currents" gallery is focused on contemporary pieces. The KMA is also home to one of the largest glass and steel assemblages in the world, created by Richard Jolley. All ages will also love the miniature Thorne Rooms on the lower level (the Art Institute of Chicago and the Phoenix Art Museum also have large collections of Thorne Rooms). Enjoy their rotating galleries that change quarterly. Open your eyes, and open your mind!

1050 World's Fair Park Dr., 865-525-6101
knoxart.org

TIP

Before perusing the gift shop, head out the balcony on the second floor for one of my favorite viewpoints of the Sunsphere!

HUNT
FOR MURALS

From large-scale projects to hidden alleys and stairwells, Knoxville's mural scene is a testament to the love of art across the city. Mural hunting is a great way to explore the city intimately, especially on foot. Whether you're into taking selfies with unique backgrounds, or you want to learn about the artists that make up the fabric of a city, hunting for murals is fun for solo travelers, couples, or the whole family. Strike a pose, jump in the air, and make some moves and some memories while you're at it! Head to the Visit Knoxville Visitors Center for a printed mural map.

visitknoxville.com/things-to-do/tours/knoxville-murals

TIP

Short on time and want to find the top five most popular murals? visitknoxville.com/blog/post/top-5-knoxville-murals

76

SEARCH FOR
SCULPTURES, STATUES, AND MEMORIALS

Enjoy art of the three-dimensional variety scattered around town by hunting for sculptures, statues, and memorials. A few must-sees are the *Tennessee Woman Suffrage Memorial* and the *Burn Memorial* (in Market Square and behind the East Tennessee History Center respectively in honor of East Tennessee's role in the 19th Amendment), *The Torchbearer* on the University of Tennessee's campus, *Rachmaninoff: The Last Concert* in World's Fair Park (the famous composer gave his last recital in Knoxville), and the *Treaty of the Holston* at Volunteer Landing. A particular favorite of mine is the *Beloved Woman of Justice* inside the Howard H. Baker Jr. Courthouse courtyard—be sure to read her accompanying plaque description. There are several sculptures in Krutch Park that change annually as part of Dogwood Arts programming.

visitknoxville.com/things-to-do/tours/statues-monuments-sculptures

77

PROCEED TO READ
WITH KNOXVILLE'S LITERARY CONNECTIONS

Famous writers may not immediately come to mind when thinking of Knoxville, but there are quite a few literary connections here. Explore the self-guided Literary Knox Walking Tour to delve into names (and related sites), including James Agee who wrote *A Death in the Family*, which was published posthumously and won a Pulitzer Prize in 1957. James Agee Park is a small park in the Fort Sanders neighborhood near where he lived in the early 1900s. Frances Hodgson Burnett wrote *The Secret Garden*, and the Knoxville Botanical Garden and Arboretum features a garden inspired by her novel. Alex Haley, famous for his novel *Roots*, lived the last years of his life just outside Knoxville. A statue and plaza in his honor resides across Morningside Park in East Knoxville. Renowned poet Nikki Giovanni grew up in Cincinnati but spent summers in Knoxville. Her poem *Knoxville* is now a children's book, and a historical marker resides on what was formerly Mulvaney Street (her essay "400 Mulvaney Street" references her grandmother's address).

James Agee Park
331 James Agee St.

Knoxville Botanical Garden and Arboretum
2743 Wimpole Ave.

Alex Haley Heritage Square
1620 Dandridge Ave.

Nikki Haley Historical Heritage Marker
Hall of Fame Dr.

literaryknox.com

HAVE A WILDLY FUN TIME
AT ZOO KNOXVILLE

Self-proclaimed “Fun on the outside, serious about animals on the inside,” Zoo Knoxville is hyperfocused on conservation of a wide variety of animal species. Known as the “Red Panda Capital of the World” for the number of these cuddly creatures they have successfully bred, they have also won awards for their efforts with saving East Tennessee’s endangered bog turtle and ongoing research with native hellbender and mudpuppy salamanders. Plan to spend time in the state-of-the-art Amphibian and Reptile Conservation Campus (ARC), Asian Trek with its Gibbon Trails and Langur Landing (Georgie the Gibbon is a ham!), and many other well-curated habitats and animals from around the world.

3500 Knoxville Zoo Dr., 865-637-5331
zooknoxville.org

TIP

Follow “Big Al” the giant Aldabra tortoise on Twitter at @bigalsays. He’s estimated to be more than 130 years old, and he’s got important stuff to say!

79

LEARN THE POWER OF PLAY
AT MUSE KNOXVILLE

For crawling tiny tots to kiddos about to hit double digits, Muse Knoxville is the perfect STEAM museum in Chilhowee Park next door to Zoo Knoxville. Children can learn science, technology, engineering, arts, and math through a variety of age-appropriate exhibits. Build with LEGOs, Rigamajig pieces, train sets, and giant blocks. Create works of art with unique materials and tools. Tone down the sensory experience in the reading nook, or put on a puppet show. Add on a visit to the planetarium, and watch the stars light up the night sky. After a trip to the Muse, your family is sure to be inspired!

516 N Beaman St., 865-594-1494
themuseknoxville.org

TIP

Don't have little ones? Experience Muse Knoxville at night with their Way Late Play Dates, and you'll feel like a kid again!

ACE THE TEST
ON THE UNIVERSITY OF TENNESSEE CAMPUS

The University of Tennessee can easily claim to be the original UT, founded in 1794, two years prior to Tennessee's statehood. Forget the University of Texas—that establishment doesn't come until 86 years later. Start with coffee at The Golden Roast to power yourself up "the Hill" and spend the morning touring campus. In addition to historic architecture, some highlights include "the Rock," Pat Summitt Plaza, and Neyland Stadium—look for the *General Neyland* statue between gates 15A and 17. After a few hours of dodging students, grab lunch beneath the lemon-hued patio umbrellas at Sunspot. Their inclusive menu will please the whole party. Spend the afternoon by strolling through the UT Gardens or perusing the McClung Museum of Natural History & Culture. For an evening out, head to the Original Copper Cellar on the Strip, so named in 1974 when 5,000 people on UT's famous Cumberland Avenue took off their clothes and, well, stripped. With that thought in mind, enjoy your dinner and then a show at the Clarence Brown Theatre.

utk.edu

QUICK STATS AND FUN FACTS

- UT has 11 colleges with over 900 programs of study.
- UT hosts 30,000-plus students from all 50 states and more than 100 countries.
- Tennessee is known as the "Volunteer State" for the large number of Tennesseans who volunteered for duty in the War of 1812, the Mexican–American War, and the Civil War; and, thus, students have been known as the "Volunteers" since the early 1900s.
- Official colors are Tennessee Orange, White, and Smokey Gray.
- Smokey is a Bluetick Coonhound and the official mascot.
- UT is only one of two universities to have a football stadium on the waterfront (University of Washington is the other).

81

ALL ABOARD!
THE THREE RIVERS RAMBLER

The Three Rivers Rambler is a train that departs downtown Knoxville, chugs along the Tennessee River to its forming point just east of downtown, and returns on a leisurely excursion. The Tennessee River is formed by the Holston and French Broad, so the three of these together make up the Three Rivers! This attraction is only available on select calendar dates throughout the year, with the most popular likely being their Christmas Lantern Express. It's a memorable holiday experience, with delightful decorations, reading, and cookies, and of course a visit from the man in red himself.

2560 University Commons Way, 865-524-9411
threeriversrambler.com

FULL SPEED AHEAD
AT THE FARRAGUT MUSEUM

The town of Farragut is the farthest western neighborhood, named after Admiral David Farragut who famously commanded "Damn the torpedoes, full speed ahead!" during the Civil War Battle of Mobile Bay. Born here, Farragut served in the War of 1812 and was a Southern Unionist who opposed secession. Today, Farragut is an affluent neighborhood with a love of water, history, and more. Dive into the Farragut Museum, boasting the largest collection related to the admiral in the country, which is an essential for Civil War or naval enthusiasts. Visitors can enjoy personal china that belonged to Farragut, alongside family photographs and manuscripts, uniform embellishments, and a nice collection of scrimshaw. The museum also tells the history of the Farragut and Concord communities. The museum features a large statue of Admiral Farragut in the front plaza, cannons on loan from the US Naval Yard, and a Civil War Trails® marker commemorating the Battle of Campbell Station fought on surrounding land in 1863.

TWIST AND TURN
ON THE FRENCH BROAD DRIVING TOUR

Before meeting the Holston River and becoming the Tennessee River, the French Broad River meanders its way from North Carolina through East Tennesse, providing a glimpse into pioneer history in a countryside setting. The French Broad Driving Tour pulls churches, historic homes and farmsteads, quarrying sites, and more into a cohesive tour of east Knox County. Start downtown and take your time winding along Riverside Drive and beyond to hit highlights including the UT Holston River Farm with its commanding views, the 1898 Gothic Revival Asbury United Methodist Church, and the 1890 Weigel House that now houses the Cruze Farm Dairy Asbury location. Get some soft serve to go and finish the tour at Seven Islands Birding Park, the only state park in Knox County and the only birding park in the state of Tennessee.

visitknoxville.com/things-to-do/tours/self-guided

BARK AND HOWL
AT MARDI GROWL

This pet-friendly town kicks it up a notch with the annual Mardi Growl Pet Parade and Festival and could be considered the start of the spring festival season. As you can guess by the name, this festival hosted by Young-Williams Animal Center happens around Mardi Gras and is a great way to push the winter doldrums to the wayside. Register your furry friend and walk in the parade, or just sit back and watch the four-legged frenzy. The festival includes animal product and service vendors, rabies shots and microchipping, and the biggest pet "pawty" around!

mardigrowl.org

CELEBRATE ARTS, CULTURE, AND NATURAL BEAUTY
WITH DOGWOOD ARTS

As the story goes, in 1947, a New York newspaper reporter wrote that "Knoxville is the ugliest city I ever saw in America." Outraging local citizens, a civic beautification project began in 1955 with the first of what would become the Dogwood Trails. Today, nonprofit organization Dogwood Arts is dedicated to celebrating arts, culture, and natural beauty in East Tennessee. Events and programs are planned year-round, but spring is the highlight—explore the Dogwood Trails by car or bike as indicated by pink stripes in select neighborhoods. Make plans to attend the juried art fair, called the Dogwood Arts Festival, in April.

dogwoodarts.com

TIP

The Dogwood Arts Chalk Walk is another annual favorite. Watch artists take squares of pavement and turn them into works of art at the beginning of April in Market Square.

86

PARTY AROUND THE GLOBE
WITHOUT LEAVING TOWN

The festivals keep rolling throughout fall in Knoxville, particularly with an international twist. The Knox Asian Festival wraps up the summer at the end of August with a menagerie of Asian cultures represented through performances, music, food, and more. HoLa Fest follows suit, celebrating Hispanic Heritage Month with pan-Latin representation in their Parade of Nations. Polka-loving partiers with stamina will want to stake out at Schulz Bräu Brewing for their three-week-long Oktoberfest, complete with stein-hoisting competitions and keg tapping on Munich time (6 a.m.!). Greek Fest is a long-running annual celebration hosted by St. George's Greek Orthodox Church just west of downtown—the perfect time for a tour of their beautiful cathedral. *Opa!*

knoxasianfestival.com
holahoralatina.org/hola-festival
schulzbraubrewing.com/events-oktoberfest
greekfesttn.com

SALUTE A SOLDIER
AT THE VETERANS DAY PARADE

The American Legion Post 2 in Knoxville has organized one of the largest Veterans Day parades in the nation since 1925. More than 100 units participate, including high school bands, local military units, community groups, and youth organizations. They also host a Memorial Day ceremony at the East Tennessee Veterans Memorial in World's Fair Park. The memorial itself is a stunning formation of 32 granite monuments bearing the inscribed names of more than 6,000 veterans from East Tennessee who have died in military service since World War I. Names and deeds of 14 Medal of Honor recipients from East Tennessee are also inscribed.

legionknox.com/veterans-day-parade

CELEBRATE CHRISTMAS IN THE CITY

It's the most wonderful time of the year . . . after football season, and after dogwood season, and, well, anytime is a wonderful time in Knoxville, but the holidays are particularly delightful. Among the parades and lighting events, there are a few events that last all season long! From the Friday after Thanksgiving to the first Sunday in the new year, partake in the Elf on the Shelf® Adventure Scavenger Hunt, where families can hunt for "scout elves" in downtown businesses with a "North Pole Pass" (fun fact: the author of *Elf on the Shelf*® graduated from the University of Tennessee!). Explore the Peppermint Trail and delight in seasonal goodies with businesses offering treats and specials like peppermint coffees, desserts, cocktails, gifts, and more. Skate under the stars in the open-air ice rink at Holidays on Ice. Throughout the season, there are dozens of events and activities guaranteed to bring holiday cheer!

knoxvilletn.gov/government/city_departments_offices/special_events/christmas_in_the_city

KEEP THE PAST ALIVE
AT THE MUSEUM OF APPALACHIA

The Museum of Appalachia is a Smithsonian Affiliate Museum in neighboring Clinton that resembles an authentic mountain farm. Visitors can expect an absolutely massive collection of artifacts (I'm talking more than 250,000 unique objects!) from residents of the Southern Appalachian region, housed among three dozen log structures. These pieces include folk art, musical instruments, quilts, Native American items, and much more. Wear comfy shoes that you don't mind getting dirty, as the collection is housed in the display barn, Hall of Fame, and several pioneer village outbuildings. You'll want to plan a few hours at least, pushing it to half a day for lunch. Exploring the property will provide a picturesque setting with which to contemplate the heritage of this region's peoples.

2819 Andersonville Hwy., Clinton, 865-494-7680
museumofappalachia.org

TIP

Plan for lunch at the museum! Their on-site restaurant serves up down-home comfort cuisine that rotates—pot roast, fried okra, garlic cheese grits, and fresh garden casserole. Yum!

DAY TRIP
TO HISTORIC CLINTON

Another city worthy of a day trip is historic Clinton, about 15 miles from downtown Knoxville. Start your day with a coffee and baked goods from E. Claire's, and plan to spend the morning doing some of the best antiquing around. Market Street and Main Street are filled with shop after shop. You'll find primitive early Americana furniture, ornate Georgian pieces, art deco, midcentury modern, recent kitschy vintage, and everything in between. A hailed lunch stop after all this shopping is Hoskins Drug Store. You'll be transported to the 1940s with their authentic soda fountain and diner fare. After lunch, jump forward a decade to the 1956 desegregation of Clinton High School. Inside the Green McAdoo Cultural Center, learn about the brave Black high schoolers known as the "Clinton 12," and others who endured anti-integration violence during the Jim Crow era and stood up for equality in education and beyond.

historicdowntownclinton.org
greenmcadoo.org

KEEP A SECRET
IN THE SECRET CITY

Just outside Knoxville lies what was once the biggest secret in the world—the city of Oak Ridge. Oak Ridge was established in 1942 as a planned city and production site for the Manhattan Project—the massive operation that developed the atomic bomb. Several facilities enriched uranium for use in Little Boy, the atomic bomb dropped on Hiroshima, Japan, in 1945. Today, many facilities are still in use as the site of the Oak Ridge National Laboratory and Y-12 National Security Complex, playing a major role in the economy and culture of the region. The story of the Manhattan Project at Oak Ridge includes historic sites and museums operated as a collaborative effort between the US Department of Energy and the National Park Service. The American Museum of Science and Energy (AMSE, a Smithsonian Affiliate Museum) offers bus tours to see this incredible slice of American history.

exploreoakridge.com
nps.gov/mapr/index.htm
amse.org/bus-tours

TIP

There are no bus tours on weekends, and the weekday tours fill up quickly. Due to the nature of these tours, all participants must be US citizens and age 10 or older.

Zoo Knoxville. Courtesy of Visit Knoxville

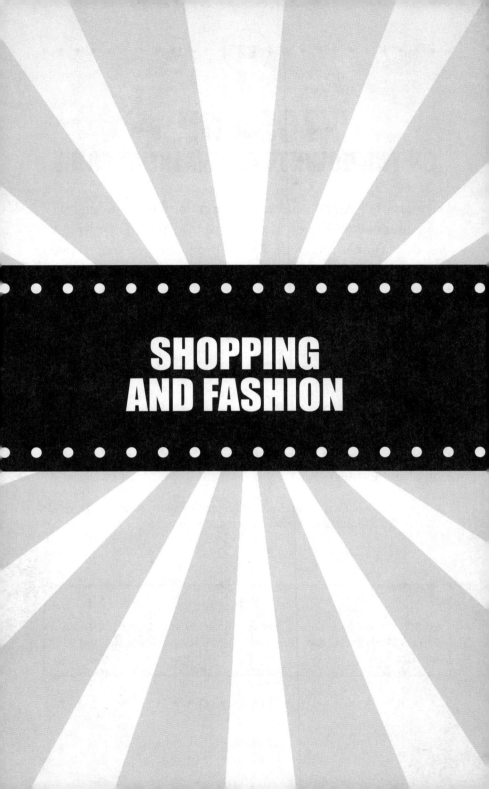

SHOPPING AND FASHION

LOOK UP
ON THE DOWNTOWN WALKING TOUR

Love history? Architecture? Wandering around with kind of a plan, but one you can do at your leisure? Then the Downtown Walking Tour is for you! This self-guided free tour created by Knox Heritage is a great way to get to know the buildings that grace the downtown streets. Both the paper guide and digital map listings provide details about each stop, including addresses, names of the buildings, and architects. It's also the perfect excuse to do some shopping, as retail options are scattered throughout. Pick up a new novel at Union Ave Books (the Daylight Building), add a Funko Pop figurine to your collection at Tall Man Toys & Comics (the Candy Factory), or buy some art to admire from the collection of artist studios at the marvelous edifice at the end of the 100 block of Gay Street (the Emporium Center).

knoxheritage.org/our-work/neighborhood-tours/
historic-downtown-knoxville-walking-tour

TIP

Look up to see the details . . . but specifically at 465 Gay Street. The Millers Department Store Building has some, er, buxom beauties at the top. Blush!

Union Ave Books
517 Union Ave., 865-951-2180
unionavebooks.com

Tall Man Toys & Comics
1060 World's Fair Park Dr., 865-219-1064
tallmantoys.com

The Emporium Center
100 S Gay St., 865-523-7543
knoxalliance.com

TAKE HEART FOR ART
ON FIRST FRIDAY

This is one of my favorite events, and, even better, it happens 12 times a year! Galleries and venues throughout the city feature artists' works for sale and live music on the fantastic evenings known as First Fridays. Many art enthusiasts start at the Emporium Center, a major anchor featuring five separate galleries that rotate monthly, alongside artist studios in the lower level. The UT Gallery is adjacent to the Emporium, and acts as an extension of the University of Tennessee on the 100 block downtown. Other popular downtown stops include the Art Market Gallery, Arrowmont Gallery, Dogwood Arts Gallery, Rala, Honeymouth, Pretentious Glass Co., and more. Stop in the Visit Knoxville Visitors Center for a monthly featured maker and free live music with the Taps & Tunes program by in-house radio station WDVX. Just north of downtown at Emory Place, you'll find two galleries side by side: Lilienthal Gallery and Pivot Point Gallery. A night out on the town while enjoying—and buying—local art? Sign me up!

The Emporium Center
100 S Gay St., 865-523-7543
knoxalliance.com

UT Gallery
106 S Gay St., 865-673-0802
downtown.utk.edu

Art Market Gallery
422 S Gay St., 865-525-5265
artmarketgallery.net

Arrowmont Gallery
110 S Gay St., 865-436-5860
arrowmont.org/arrowmont-gallery

Dogwood Arts Gallery
123 W Jackson Ave., 865-637-4561
dogwoodarts.com/dogwoodgallery

Rala
112 W Jackson Ave., 865-525-7888
shoprala.com

Honeymouth
125 S Central St., 865-240-3956
shophoneymouth.com

Pretentious Glass Co.
133 S Central St., 865-249-8677
pretentiousglassco.com

Visit Knoxville
301 S Gay St., 865-523-7263
visitknoxville.com

Lilienthal Gallery
23 Emory Pl., 865-200-4401
lilienthalgallery.com

Pivot Point Gallery
15 Emory Pl., 865-248-0050
pivotpointgallery.com

MAKE HASTE
TO THE MAKER CITY

In 2016, Etsy chose Knoxville as one of 13 cities to host one of their first Maker City Summits, and Knoxville has had the nickname of "the Maker City" ever since. Many artisans and makers call Knoxville home, which continues a long line of craftsmanship throughout the Appalachians, and there are more than 900 represented with the Maker City. Today, savvy shoppers can get to know the maker community at events such as the Retropolitan Craft Fairs, Old City Markets, the Foothills Craft Guild, Old Sevier Sunday Markets, and more throughout the year. Shops like Rala (Regional and Local Artisans), Jacks of Knoxville, the Southern Market, Honeymouth, and even the Visit Knoxville Visitors Center carry a multitude of items handmade by artisans across the region.

themakercity.org

TIP

The Maker City's website is a great resource—explore their directory to find new artisans and their products!

95

SHOP FROM YESTERYEAR
AT MAST GENERAL STORE

General stores were once the kind of shops that serviced the community's needs from cradle to grave. The Mast General Store was such a place, and the original one opened in the rural community of Valle Crucis, North Carolina, in 1883. Out of the ashes of Knoxville's infamous Million Dollar Fire in 1897 comes the building that now houses another Mast General Store, built the following year in 1898. At that time, it was home to the McNulty Grocery and Dry Goods Co., followed by several more general and department stores until the late 1980s. After a few decades of being used for storage, the Mast Store opened in this building in 2006. Shoppers can find clothing, outdoors gear, toys, specialty Southern food items, gifts, and of course their barrels filled to the brim with old-fashioned candies.

402 S Gay St., 865-546-1336
mastgeneralstore.com/knoxville

GET GROOVY
AT KNOXVILLE'S VINTAGE STORES

Vintage, retro, and midcentury modern are all the rage, and Knoxville has more than enough to light your lava lamp. Spend a day throwing it back a few decades. Retrospect in North Knoxville and Nostalgia in Bearden both have everything a disco diva could need from stereo equipment to bell bottoms. Fashionistas will want to visit Pioneer House to please their inner rhinestone cowboy, including vintage boots, fringe, letterpress art, and turquoise belt buckles. For '80s and '90s lovers, French Fried Vintage has the perfect retro garb to make you forget your parents never paid extra for the laser background in your first-grade school photos. Looking to match your decor to *Mad Men*? Mid Mod Collective has midcentury modern, Danish modern, and industrial furniture and art waiting for you to take them home.

Retrospect
1121 N Central St., 865-522-3511
facebook.com/retrospectvintagestore

Nostalgia
5214 Homberg Dr., 865-584-0832
facebook.com/nostalgiaknoxville

Pioneer House
(by appointment only)
700 E Depot Ave., 865-405-8275
pioneer-house.com

French Fried Vintage
7 Emory Pl., 865-599-8556
facebook.com/frenchfriedvintage

Mid Mod Collective
1621 N Central St., 865-337-5575
midmodcollective.com

TO MARKET, TO MARKET
IN MARKET SQUARE

Market Square is the heart of downtown, and its history spans multiple decades. William Swan and Joseph Mabry (of Mabry-Hazen House) were two savvy developers in the mid-1800s. In 1854, they donated land to the city for a public market, wisely raising the adjacent property values along the way. By 1870, the Knoxville History Project notes it already looked similar to how it is today with two rows of buildings framing the square. The square has seen many changes in its century-and-a-half span, and today's visitors to Market Square can enjoy boutique shopping, restaurants (patio season is the best!), rooftop drinks, live music, the Market Square Farmers Market, and year-round events and festivals.

Earth to Old City
22 Market Sq., 865-522-8270
earthtooldcity.com

Fizz
27 Market Sq., 865-851-7990
fizzmarketsquare.com

Fruit Jar Alley
23 Market Sq., 423-532-8499
fruitjaralley.shop

Proper Popcorn
29 Market Sq., 865-381-2929
properpopcorn.com

GO WEST, YOUNG MAN,
TO WEST KNOXVILLE

West Knoxville is a broad section of town that could include Bearden and Farragut, but narrowing it down to thinking of this area as anchored by West Town Mall and Turkey Creek shopping centers is easiest. In addition to big-box shopping, boutiques and locally owned restaurants are scattered throughout. Start with coffee and a bagel at K Brew, and then spend your morning in a retail therapy session. Women's fashion stores Bliss and CJ's Closet are in West Town, and Val's Boutique (another women's fashion store), Bradley's Gift & Home (they make their own chocolates), Hound Dogs of Knoxville (all kinds of University of Tennessee gear—go Vols!), Painted Tree Boutiques (a warehouse-sized booth-style mall full of clothing, home decor, and more), and Liz Beth & Co. (a beautiful art gallery) are all along Kingston Pike. Sports lovers can head back to the mall for Dick's House of Sport—one of only three in the country (the original in Rochester, New York, and the latest in Minnetonka, Minnesota).

SHOP 'TIL YOU DROP
IN BEARDEN

Bearden is an eclectic neighborhood west of downtown and difficult to define. Start at Holly's Gourmet Market & Cafe. Follow with shopping Bearden's high-end art galleries and interior design: Persian Galleries, Bennett Galleries, the District Gallery & Framery, Todd Richesin Interiors, Laws Interiors, Art Galleria, G&G Interiors, and more. Antique hunters should peruse Bearden Antique Mall and Blair House Antiques. When you need to stop for a refresher, Knoxville's a place where a midafternoon beer is totally in order.

Bearden Beer Market offers a huge selection of cans and bottles or do a flight at Abridged Beer Co. Head down Homberg for the Southern Market, Jerry's Artarama, and Nostalgia; then to Kingston Pike for the DW Designs offering soft tees; Est8te, Elle, and Obligato for upscale trendy pieces; and Fig & Co., Ironic, and the Back Porch Mercantile for decor. Outdoor lovers will be hooked by 3 Rivers Angler where you can pick up fly-fishing goodies or book a guided fishing trip to explore. End the evening with Bistro by the Tracks or Harvest.

Persian Galleries
4461 Kingston Pike, 865-558-8777
persiangalleriesknoxville.com

Bennett Galleries
5308 Kingston Pike, 865-584-6791
bennetthome.com

The District Gallery & Framery
5113 Kingston Pike, 865-200-4452
thedistrictgallery.com

Todd Richesin Interiors
4514 Kingston Pike, 865-249-6612
toddrichesininteriors.com

Laws Interiors
4610 Kingston Pike, 865-584-1400
lawsinteriors.com

Art Galleria
6703 Kingston Pike, 865-583-0044
artgalleriaknoxville.com

G&G Interiors
5508 Kingston Pike, 865-212-5639
gg-interiors.com

Bearden Antique Mall
310 S Mohican St., 865-584-1521
facebook.com/beardenantiques

Blair House Antiques
210 N Forest Park Blvd.
865-584-8119
blairhouseantiquesknoxville.com

The Southern Market
5400 Homberg Dr., 865-588-0274
southernmarketonline.com

Jerry's Artarama
5220 Homberg Dr., 865-588-0738
jerrysartarama.com

Nostalgia
5214 Homberg Dr., 865-584-0832
facebook.com/nostalgiaknoxville

The DW Designs
5209 Kingston Pike, 865-951-1983
thedwdesigns.com

Est8te
5609 Kingston Pike, 865-588-1588
est8te.com

Elle
5508 Kingston Pike, 865-606-5449
shopelleboutique.com

Obligato
4626 Kingston Pike, 865-558-0822
obligatoknoxville.com

Fig & Co.
5072 Kingston Pike, 865-357-3363
figandcompany.com

Ironic
5054 Kingston Pike, 865-588-3131
shopironicknox.com

The Back Porch Mercantile
5440 Homberg Dr., 865-247-4532
thebackporchmercantile.com

3 Rivers Angler
5113 Kingston Pike
865-200-5271
3riversangler.com

SNEAK THROUGH
SUTHERLAND AVENUE

Sutherland isn't a main drag like Kingston Pike, but it runs parallel to Kingston in the Bearden neighborhood; although Sutherland is a bit removed, it holds its own. Backroads Market carries Maryville's Vienna Coffee Co. alongside farmhouse-style home decor. Lots of local- and niche-interest shopping can be done here. Aimee's Bohemian Jewelry & Imports offers south/southeast Asian attire and gifts. Pop into the Long Run, catering to runners and yogis. Head to River Sports Outfitters for hiking, biking, climbing, and kayaking gear, and also enjoy their climbing wall. If you'd rather stay on the ground, John Tarleton Park has several soccer and football fields, and a playground, with Third Creek Greenway access nearby, connecting to several other greenways.

Backroads Market
514 Walker St., 865-525-9412
backroadsmarketknox.com

Aimee's Bohemian Jewelry & Imports
2610 Sutherland Ave., 865-546-2333
facebook.com/aimees.bohemian

The Long Run
2452 Sutherland Ave., 865-851-7874
thelongrun865.com

River Sports Outfitters
2918 Sutherland Ave., 865-523-0066
riversportsoutfitters.com

Dogwood. Courtesy of Visit Knoxville

ACTIVITIES BY SEASON

SPRING

Tell a Secret at the Knoxville Botanical Garden, 58
Bark and Howl at Mardi Growl, 105
Listen Up at Big Ears, 47
Celebrate Arts, Culture, and Natural Beauty with Dogwood Arts, 106
Open Up to the Opera at the Rossini Festival, 48

SUMMER

Cruise the Tennessee River, 63
Catch a Skyline Sunset from a Rooftop Bar, 14
Fill Your Tote Bag at the Market Square Farmers Market, 18
Pack a Picnic at UT Gardens, 60

FALL

Sing "Rocky Top" at a UT Football Game, 52
Party around the Globe without Leaving Town, 108
Be Merry and Go Round at the Tennessee Valley Fair, 49
Salute a Soldier at the Veterans Day Parade, 109
Be A-MAZE-D at Maple Lane Farms, 72

WINTER

Sip in a Swing at K Brew, 20
Shout "Let's Go, Ice Bears!" at a Knoxville Ice Bears Hockey Game, 56
Watch the Process at Pretentious Craft Co., 30
All Aboard! The Three Rivers Rambler, 102
Celebrate Christmas in the City, 110

HoLa Fest. Courtesy of Visit Knoxville

Adeem the Artist. Courtesy of Ed Rode

SUGGESTED ITINERARIES

NATURE-LOVING

Head into the Urban Wilderness, 53
Paddle the Tennessee River, 62
Take a Hike at House Mountain, 69
All Aboard! The Three Rivers Rambler, 102
Taste Tennessee at Tsali Notch Winery, 31
Do It Your Way in the Great Smoky Mountains National Park, 73

ADVENTURE-SEEKING

Find Your Favorite BBQ, 2
Traverse the Ale Trail, 12
Go Your Own Way on a Greenway, 55
Divide and Conquer on the Civil War Driving Tour, 90
Listen Up at Big Ears, 47

ARTSY-KINDA-TOWN

Get Down at the Clarence Brown Theatre, 36
Follow Your (He)Art at Historic Westwood, 83
Carve Out an Afternoon at Candoro Marble Building, 87
Take Heart for Art on First Friday, 118
Celebrate Arts, Culture, and Natural Beauty with Dogwood Arts, 106

ON A BUDGET

Rock Out at the School of Music, 42
Hunt for Murals, 94
Be One with Nature at Ijams Nature Center, 54
Fiddle Around on the Cradle of Country Music Tour, 43
Go Back Further in Time at the McClung Museum, 85

ONLY IN KNOXVILLE

Have a Nice Day at the Nicest Place in America, 10
Hoot 'n' Holler at the WDVX Blue Plate Special, 39
Shoot Hoops at the Women's Basketball Hall of Fame, 57
Wig Out at the Sunsphere, 88
Watch the Process at Pretentious Craft Co., 30

RAINY DAY

Go Back in Time at the East Tennessee History Center, 84
Open Your Eyes at the Knoxville Museum of Art, 93
Shop from Yesteryear at Mast General Store, 121
Preserve African American History at the Beck Cultural Exchange Center, 86

FOODIE FAVORITES

Go from Farm to Table, 6
Eat Your Way through Knoxville on a Food Tour, 19
Dance a Jig at Boyd's Jig and Reel, 38
Party around the Globe without Leaving Town, 108

FUN WITH KIDS

Swing through the Trees at Navitat, 65

Scream for Ice Cream at the Phoenix Pharmacy and Cruze Farm, 17

Learn the Power of Play at Muse Knoxville, 99

Break a Leg at the Knoxville Children's Theatre, 37

Have a Wildly Fun Time at Zoo Knoxville, 98

OFF THE BEATEN PATH

Take a Hike at House Mountain, 69

Sneak through Sutherland Avenue, 128

Have a Bonny Good Time at Marble Springs, 78

Proceed to Read with Knoxville's Literary Connections, 96

Think Pink (or Blue) at Historic Ramsey House, 80

DATE NIGHT

Consume Cocktails in Concealment, 25

Spare an Afternoon at Maple Hall, 64

Dust Off Your Spurs at Lonesome Dove, 22

Give Regards to Broadway at the Tennessee Theatre, 34

Tune into the Knoxville Symphony Orchestra, 44

Mountain Biking in Knoxville's
Urban Wilderness. Courtesy of Dawn Majors

INDEX

3 Rivers Angler, 126–127
A Dopo, 26–27
Abridged Beer Co., 13, 126
Aimee's Bohemian Jewelry & Imports, 128–129
Albright Grove, 13
Ale' Rae's Gastropub, 26–27
Ale Trail, 12–13, 26
Alex Haley Statue, 96
Alliance Brewing Company, 13, 28–29
American Museum of Science and Energy, 113
Archers BBQ, 3
Arrowmont Gallery, 118–119
Art Galleria, 126–127
Art Market Gallery, 118–119
Back Porch Mercantile, 126–127
Baker Creek Preserve, 53
Barley's Taproom & Pizzeria, 39
Bearden, 19, 66, 68, 122, 125, 126–127, 128
Bearden Antique Mall, 126–127
Bearden Beer Market, 126
Beck Cultural Exchange Center, 86
Bennett Galleries, 126–127
Bernadette's Crystal Gardens, 14–15
Bethel Cemetery, 82
Bida Saigon, 8–9
Big Ears, 47
Bijou Theatre, 32, 35, 44, 79
Bistro by the Tracks, 126
Blair House Antiques, 126–127
Bliss, 125
Blossom Bowls, 26–27
Blount Mansion, 77
Boyd's Jig and Reel, 8–9, 38
Bradley's Gift & Home, 125
Brazeiros, 8–9
Candoro Marble Building, 87
Capybara Coffee, 20–21
Carpetbag Theatre, 45
Cave at Hey Bear Cafe, The, 4
Central Cinema, 46
Central Filling Station, 4
Chalk Walk, 107
Cherohala Skyway, 31
Cherokee Caverns, 92

Chilhowee Park, 49, 67, 99
Chivo Taqueria, 19
Civil War Driving Tour, 90
CJ's Closet, 125
Clancy's, 8–9
Clarence Brown Theatre, The, 36, 100
Clinton, 111, 112
Club XYZ, 46
CommonPlace Coffee, 28–29
Copper Cellar, 100
Cove at Concord Park, 62
Cradle of Country Music Tour, 43
Crafty Bastard Brewery, 13, 26–27
Crescent Bend, 79, 83
Cruze Farm Ice Cream, 17
Dead End BBQ, 2–3
Dick's House of Sport, 125
District Gallery & Framery, The, 126–127
Dogwood Arts, 95, 106–107, 118–119
Dogwood Trails, 106
Donut Shop, The, 26–27
Downtown Walking Tour, 116
Drawing Room, The, 24
DW Designs, The, 126–127
East Knoxville, 17, 58, 86, 96
East Tennessee History Center, 84, 87, 95
Elf on the Shelf® Adventure Scavenger Hunt, 110
Elle, 126–127
Elst Brewing Company, 13
Embassy Suites, 14
Emilia, 8–9
Emporium Center, The, 116–117, 118–119
Est8te, 126–127
Everly Brothers Park, 66
Fanatic Brewing Company, 13
Farragut, 14, 103, 125
Farragut Museum, 103
Fig & Co., 126–127
Fin Two Japanese Ale House, 19
First Friday, 39, 118
Five Thirty Lounge, 14–15
Fort Dickerson, 53
French Fried Vintage, 122–123
French Market Crêperie, The, 8–9
G&G Interiors, 126–127
Geezers Brewery, 13, 27
Golden Roast, The, 20–21, 100
Good Golly Tamale, 19
Gosh Ethiopian Restaurant, 8–9
Graduate Knoxville, The, 23

Great Smoky Mountains National Park, 73, 79
Greek Fest, 108
Green McAdoo Cultural Center, 112
greenways, 53, 55, 61, 68, 128
Gypsy Circus Barrelhouse, 26
Happy Holler, 4, 46
Harvest, 126
High Ground Park, 53
Historic Ramsey House, 80
Historic Westwood, 83
Hi-Wire Brewing Taproom, 28–29
HoLa Festival, 108
Holidays on Ice, 110
Holly's Gourmet Market & Cafe, 126
Honeybee Coffee, 20–21, 28–29
Honeymouth, 118–119, 120
House Mountain, 69
Hyatt Place Hotel, 14
Ijams Nature Center, 54, 65
Jackie's Dream, 5, 26–27
Jacks of Knoxville, 120
James Agee Park, 96–97
James White's Fort, 74, 76
J. C. Holdway, 6
Jerry's Artarama, 126–127
John Tarleton Park, 128
K Brew, 20–21, 125
Kaizen, 8–9
Kefi, 8–9
Knox Asian Festival, 108
Knox Brew Hub, 12
Knox Brew Tours, 12
Knox Whiskey Works, 16
Knoxville Adventure Collective, 50, 55, 61, 62
Knoxville Botanical Garden and Arboretum, 44, 58, 60, 87, 97
Knoxville Children's Theatre, 37, 46
Knoxville Convention Center, 89
Knoxville Food Tours, 19
Knoxville Ice Bears, 56
Knoxville Jazz Orchestra, 35
Knoxville Museum of Art, 87, 93
Knoxville Opera, 34, 48
Knoxville Symphony Orchestra, 34, 35, 44
Knoxville Walking Tours, 91
KoPita, 8–9
Krutch Park, 95
Lakeshore Park, 68
Landing House, The, 8–9, 28–29
Laws Interiors, 126–127

Lilienthal Gallery, 118–119
Liz Beth & Co., 125
Lonesome Dove, 22
Long Run, The, 108, 128–129
Lost & Found Records, 26–27
Lunch House, 5
Mabry-Hazen House, 55, 82, 86, 124
Main Event, 72
Maple Hall, 64
Maple Lane Farms, 72
Marble Springs, 78
Mardi Growl, 105
Market Square, 6, 7, 8, 14, 18, 44, 95, 107, 124
Market Square Farmers Market, 18, 124
Mast General Store, 121
McClung Historical Collection, 84
McClung Museum of Natural History & Culture, 85, 100
Mid Mod Collective, 122–123
Morningside Park, 96
murals, 20, 23, 94
Muse Knoxville, 67, 99
Museum of Appalachia, 111
Myrtle's Chicken & Beer, 19
Nama, 8–9
Navitat, 65
Next Level Brewing Company, 13, 26–27
Neyland Stadium, 23, 52, 55, 100
North Knoxville, 19, 26, 46, 122
Northshore Brasserie, 8–9
Nostalgia, 122–123, 126–127
Oak Ridge, 113
Oak Room by Abridged, The, 12–13
Oakwood BBQ, 2–3
Obligato, 126–127
Oglewood Avenue, 26–27
Old Gray Cemetery, 26–27
OliBea, 6
Oliver Royale, 6
One Knoxville Sporting Club, 70
Painted Tree Boutiques, 125
Pat Summitt Plaza, 100
Paysan Bread & Bagels, 26–27
Peppermint Trail, 110
Persian Galleries, 126–127
Peter Kern Library, 25
Pete's Restaurant, 5
Petro's Chili & Chips, 7
Phoenix Pharmacy & Fountain, The, 17
Pioneer House, 122–123

Pivot Point Gallery, 118–119
Pop Weasel Emporium, 26–27
PostModern Spirits, 16
Preservation Pub, 14–15
Pretentious Beer & Glass Co., 12, 13, 30
Printshop Beer Co., 13, 28–29
Radius Rooftop Lounge, 14–15
Rala, 118–119, 120
Rami's Cafe, 26–27
Redbud Kitchen, 28–29
Remedy Coffee, 26–27
Retrospect, 122–123
River & Rail Theatre, 41
River Bluff Wildlife Area, 53
River Sports Outfitters, 62, 128–129
Rossini Festival, 48
Round Up Restaurant, 5
Rubik's Cube, 89
Saloon 16, 23, 24
Savelli's, 8–9
School of Music, 42
Schulz Bräu, 12–13, 108
Scruffy City Hall, 14–15
Sharp's Ridge Veteran's Memorial Park, 26–27
Simpl., 28–29
Sitar, 8–9
SoKno Taco, 28–29
South Coast Pizza, 28–29
South Knoxville, 2, 28, 87
South Press, 28–29
Southern Grit, 19
Southern Market, 120, 126–127
SouthSide Garage, 4
statues, 57, 85, 95, 96, 100, 103
Sticky Rice Cafe, 8–9
Sunsphere, 24, 88, 93
Surin of Thailand, 8–9
Sutherland Avenue, 128
Suttree Landing Park, 53
Sweet P's BBQ, 2–3
Tall Man Toys & Comics, 116–117
Tandur, 8–9
Taqueria La Herradura, 8–9, 26–27
TENNESSEAN Personal Luxury Hotel, THE, 24
Tennessee Association of Vintage Base Ball, 81
Tennessee River, 24, 41, 53, 61, 62, 63, 68, 79, 102, 104
Tennessee Riverboat, 63
Tennessee Smokies, 71
Tennessee Theatre, The, 34, 35, 44

Tennessee Valley Fair, 49, 67
Tennessee Whiskey Trail, 16
Theatre Knoxville Downtown, 40
Three Rivers Rambler, 102
Todd Richesin Interiors, 126–127
Tonya Rea's Teas & Remedies, 26–27
Tsali Notch Winery, 31
Turkey Creek, 125
Union Ave Books, 116–117
University of Tennessee (UT), 20, 22, 23, 30, 36, 42, 52, 60, 71, 85, 95, 100–101, 104, 110, 118, 125
Urban Wilderness, 20, 53, 54, 55, 65
UT Gallery, 118–119
UT Gardens, 60, 100
Val's Boutique, 125
Vault, The, 25
Veterans Day Parade, 109
Vida, 25
Visit Knoxville, 39, 88, 94, 118–119, 120
Volunteer Princess, 63
WDVX, 39, 118
West Knoxville, 4, 125
West Town Mall, 125
Wild Love Bakehouse, 20–21
Women's Basketball Hall of Fame, 57
World's Fair Park, 44, 88, 95, 109
Xül Beer Company, 13, 26–27
Yassin's Falafel House, 8–9, 10
Zoo Knoxville, 98, 99, 114